设计对话

DESIGN DIALOGUES
INTERVIEWS WITH FAMOUS
ASIAN-PACIFIC DESIGNERS

——亚太名师访谈

深圳视界文化传播有限公司 编

中国林业出版社
China Forestry Publishing House

During the design process, the important thing is the endless development.

As life changes, designers should change the ways of expression, shoulder the responsibilities, and take more challenges.

All the time, we are actively planning a book about the interviews with famous designers.

Through interviewing with forerunners, we can gain some ideas, insights and experiences from them.

It is a great honor to get responses from a large number of famous designers after our invitations.

This book consists of their sincerest expressions of design, which can give us a deep understanding of what is the real design.

Meanwhile, the stories of designing life and life design are very wonderful.

It is also very regrettable that we only choose a part of famous designers as representatives because of the limited pages.

Our ultimate hope is that good designs will always be presented to everyone for the first time.

在设计工作中

重要的是不断地发展

随着生活的变化而改变表现方式

担负起重任

迎接更多的挑战

一直以来

我们都在积极策划一本设计名师访谈的书籍

希望通过与前辈们的对话

获得一些理念、感悟和经验

很荣幸

这次

在我们发出邀请之后

得到众多设计名师的回应

本书收录的皆是他们最真诚的设计表达

给我们深刻的认识

什么是真正的设计

设计生活与生活设计的故事

很精彩

同时也非常遗憾

因为书籍篇幅有限

我们只能选取一部分作为代表

我们最终的希望是

好的设计

永远第一时间呈现给大家

名家索引

THE FAMOUS
DESIGNERS' INDEX

008

040

064

09

124

158

168

19

202

222

234

246

260

270

278

290

目录 CONTENTS

戴勇

Eric Tai

独具特色的"中国式优雅"

戴勇室内设计师事务所 创始人
卡萨艺术品有限公司 董事长、设计总监

获得荣誉

中国当代最具影响力的室内设计师之一

出版了《极上雅境》《中国式优雅》《融会》
等八本个人作品集

2012年 受聘清华美术学院高级室内设计研修班授课教师

2009年 获颁"中国十大设计师"称号

2009年 作品入选国际室内设计奥斯卡英国AndrewMartin
安德鲁马丁奖

2004年 作品"佳兆业桂芳园样板房"荣获海峡两岸四地
设计大奖一等奖等

近些年新中式风格非常流行，您设计的项目也以中式居多，如深圳自己的家与事务所都是以简约中式为主，是个人比较喜欢中式风格吗？

戴勇： 从去年到今年我把自己的工作和生活重新定义了一下，搬了办公室，搬了新家。在设计办公室和新家的时候，有以前买的的一些家具和一些画作，有现代的，也有偏中式的。主要是根据这些现有的物品做了归纳，办公室偏现代一些，家里偏中式一些。办公室里的物品是偏西方的，有一些北欧的家具及摆件；家里的物品是偏东方的，如古典的中式家具及器物。居住空间里的陈设也是有过去有现在，有新有旧，舒适实用就好了。

对中国优秀传统文化有没有特别的情节？

戴勇： 我对中国文化的认识更多是来源于上学时候的绘画经历，画了十多年国画，也练了多年书法。这种情节是潜移默化的，性情上的改变是终身的。对于遇到的一些人和事，我越来越不想评论，宁愿避而远之，修身养性才对设计更有帮助。熟悉我的朋友会看的出来，我们的设计是节制的，也是丰富的，更是中国的。

您最新的作品"康桥悦蓉园新中式院墅"被很多业界设计师赞赏，尤其是那抹红色，雅而不俗，可谓经典。当初设计这个项目的定位是什么？背后有什么故事吗？

戴勇： 我们17年每个月都会发表一个新的作品，每个作品各有特色。"悦蓉园"项目是8月份发表的项目，是郑州康桥地产的一个现代中式定位的楼盘。"悦蓉园"的硬装是比较理性严谨的系统，软装是布鲁盟公司执行的，加入了许多感性的元素，给人一种外放的视觉感受。在后期完工照片拍摄时，我们也做了很多减法，尽可能收一些。设计本身来说，如果能表达出更多的不同，每个设计师发挥自己的个性，去做出不一样的表达，也是一种很好的尝试。

那么东方设计与西方设计在表达上有什么不一样？

戴勇： 舍而不露是东方设计的一个特点，中国人喜欢委婉，东方设计具有的含蓄美感与西方大胆热烈的表达方式在本质上就有所区别。中式讲究意境，在设计中蕴含一种淡然悠远的人文气韵，让人感觉到民族深厚的文化气质和亲和力。

您的助理说您特别喜欢摄影，是因为做设计本身的情感原因吗？

戴勇：是的，我玩摄影已经二十多年了，很早前的设计项目完成后都是自己拍完工照片，曾经帮设计师朋友拍的项目还荣获过亚太设计大奖。台湾摄影师莫尚勤是我最早的摄影启蒙老师，近几年，我一直把自己的摄影作品用在自己的设计项目中，也得到了客户的认可。今年，我的摄影作品已由深圳星创家居代理，在国际品牌Stellar Works深圳艺展中心专卖店里公开发售。

优秀的摄影作品是有灵魂的，优秀的设计作品同样有灵性，摄影和设计都是通过视觉效果去传递思想的一种方式。

您会把您看到或者拍到的东西，融入到设计中吗？

戴勇：会，其实灵感这个东西无处不在，不仅是摄影，生活中更是随处可见，但是要怎么样去抓住它并把它转化为现实，我认为需要不断地去思考去实践。

中国室内设计行业飞速发展，让更多的中国本土设计师成长起来，并有机会在国际舞台上展现我们中国的风采，2009年您就作为深圳首位获选英国Andrew Martin室内设计奥斯卡全球优秀室内设计师，有什么感想吗？

戴勇：继续前行，不断进步吧！设计师的水准永远是山外有山天外有天，安于现状和骄傲自大都不行的，要保持设计的思维一直坚持下去，与时俱进，在积累中获得更多的实践经验与灵感。不忘初心，方得始终。

其实以您现在设计名师的地位，在业界应该非常活跃才对，却很少见您自己曝光在大众视野，为什么呢？是性格使然吗？

戴勇：是不是设计名师，都是别人说的，我每天做的事都是以一个普通设计师的标准在要求自己。每个人有自己的生活方式，我只是一名室内设计师，设计师每天应该忙的是跟设计及创意有关的事情。

另外，设计事务的确很多，给家人的时间本来就很少，除了工作之外我仅有的时间愿意都是给家人的。设计师不是明星，我也不是营销型设计师，不需要很多的曝光率，我只是把设计工作做好，跟设计无关的事会尽可能避而远之。从个人性格方面，我也

不喜欢应酬，也推掉了很多商业活动及讲课，这种远离喧嚣的设计圈的生活方式挺适合我。

这几年合作下来，您一直是非常积极致力于出版的，是因为对书籍的喜爱吗？或者对于设计师出版有没有什么益处？

戴勇：一直以来，我希望做的是一种可以持续的事，并会持续产生一种作用，时间越久，作用越大。在这个想法驱使下，我会选择专注把设计做好，设计做好了，我们的客户会越稳定，也越来越多。包括我们选择专注做好作品，好的完工项目越来越多，结集出版，也是水到渠成的事。

一个设计品牌，需要有自己的作品书籍展示并证明自己的设计能力，作品专辑是最基本的，也是最传统的展示方式。我们的设计书籍也很畅销，相信对行业来说是一种正面的力量，对年轻设计师会有一种激励的作用。

您自己出版了很多本作品集，除此之外，有哪本您特别珍藏的设计图书吗？为什么？

戴勇：我们共出了8本设计作品集，最后一本是2016年出版的，虽然设计图书市场萎缩，但是这本书反而是卖的最好的，并二次加印。我一直都有买纸版设计书的习惯，每个月都会买设计书。做的好的设计书也很多，如Kerry Hill、Jaya、陈幼坚的作品专辑等，都是难得的好书。

设计师多读书的好处可以跟我们分享一下吗？

戴勇：阅读更多的是带来思考，建立起自己的思维模式，知识面的广度决定了思维的活跃程度，设计师其实就是解决问题的人，活跃的思维可以帮助你在面对问题时，如何在最短的时间内找到最合理的解决方案。

对于年轻一代设计师，他们现在最应该要做的是什么？可以指点一二吗？

戴勇：对于设计师，不管是年轻的，还是年老的，都要不断地多出作品，出好作品，尽早完成自己的第一本设计作品集。

极致美 东方墅

THE EXTREME BEAUTY OF ORIENTAL VILLA

项目名称 | 建业比华利庄园别墅样板房

室内设计 | 戴勇室内设计师事务所（深圳）

陈设软装 | 戴勇室内设计师事务所（深圳）

项目地点 | 河南新乡

项目面积 | 280 ㎡

主要材料 | 布拉格灰云石、山水纹云石、胡桃木饰面、橡木地板、墙纸、布艺等

摄 影 师 | B+M Studio陈彦铭

设计理念 | DESIGN CONCEPT

The project is located in the north of Phoenix Lake in Zhengzhou, and the livable Yellow River Wetland strives to create the new territory of international top leisure resort. Through the perfect division of spatial functions, the designer uses simple Oriental delicate aesthetics as an extension of the design to create a spatial experience with an extraordinary atmosphere.

The spatial planning of the foyer achieves the dual functions of storage and display well. The overall design of the living room strongly presents the elegant, delicate, and quiet power of the villa space. The bookshelf design full of the wall as a facade of a powerful spiritual carrier, allocating with ink painting make the whole space generous, dignified, accessible and knowledgeable. The symmetrical structure of space, the usage of materials and the furnishing way of soft decorations reflect the charm and sense of ceremony of Chinese style. In the Oriental aesthetics having been mentioned today, this case shows an open attitude and maintains its style.

The living room is high-raised, and the sitting room on the second floor faces the downstairs. The dining room not only extends the implicit and elegant lifestyle and etiquette but also refines the classical elements for simplifying and enriching. The circular solid dining table is more concise and smooth, and the humanized layout collocation with the top textured materials creates a quiet and comfortable dining space.

本项目位于北郑州凤湖畔，黄河湿地畔品质宜居千亩大盘，着力打造国际顶级休闲度假新领地。设计师通过空间功能的完美划分，以简约东方的精致美学作为设计的延伸，打造出气质非凡的空间体验。

入口玄关的空间规划恰到好处地实现了储藏和展示的双重功能。客厅整体设计极力呈现别墅空间雅致、安静的力量。满墙书架式设计作为立面极具震撼力的精神载体，搭配水墨挂画让整体空间大气凝远、通达而有识鉴。空间对称的结构、材质的运用及软装陈列方式都体现出中式的韵味与仪式感。在东方美学被不断提起的今天，呈现出一种开放的姿态，并保持自我的风格。

客厅中空挑高，二楼起居室与楼下对望。餐厅设计不仅延续了含蓄、高雅的生活方式与礼制之道，提炼出经典元素加以简化和丰富，圆形实木餐桌更显简约与流畅，人性化布局搭配触感顶级的材质，营造安静、舒适的用餐空间。

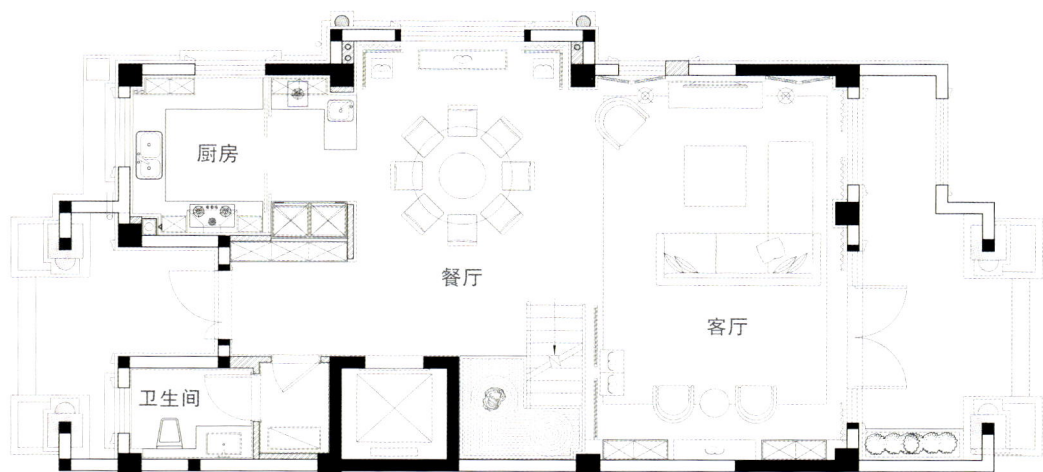

厨房

餐厅

客厅

卫生间

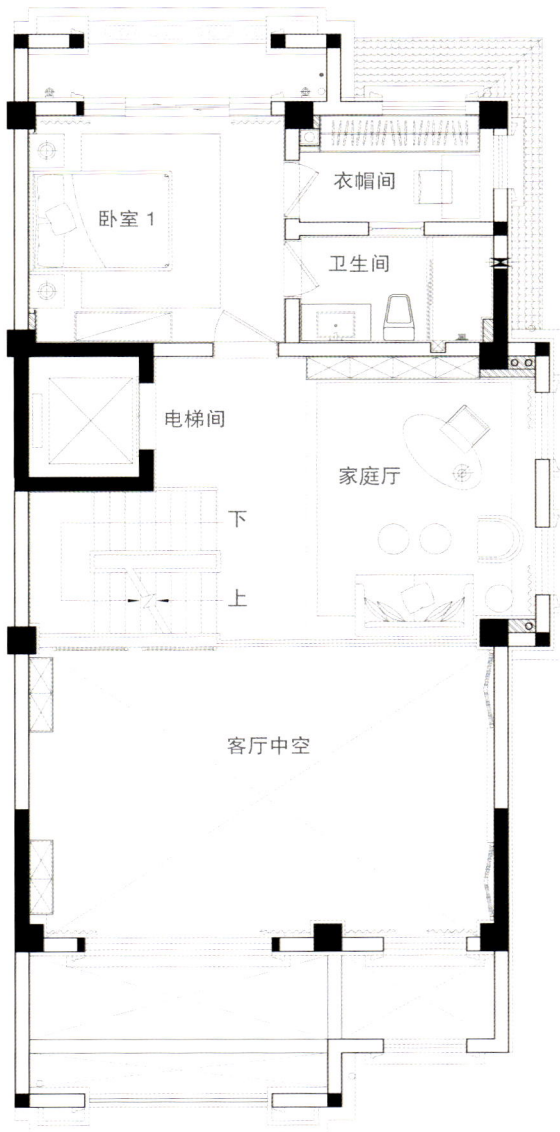

衣帽间

卫生间

卧室1

电梯间

家庭厅

下

上

客厅中空

The second floor is the elder's room and family entertainment area, which continue with the pace of the whole space. The master bedroom is the biggest highlight of this case. The background wall of bedroom selects the slat as vertical segmentation, and the concise and clear wooden grille, fashionable and steady furniture and the warm lighting atmosphere make space warm, comfortable, elegant and noble. The ceiling design uses the inclined roof shape, which is generous and stable. The soft textured wood, the light, elegant and plain colors, and the embellishment of arts create a new orientation for the master bedroom. Setting a tea tasting area at terrace can excavate more possibilities of a life interest, and tasting the tea, enjoying the scenery can reflect a calm and natural atmosphere.

In this mansion full of humanistic feelings, through every detail of life, one can feel the design give life more quality and meaning. The aesthetic feeling together with functions achieves the noble, elegant and delicate ideal life.

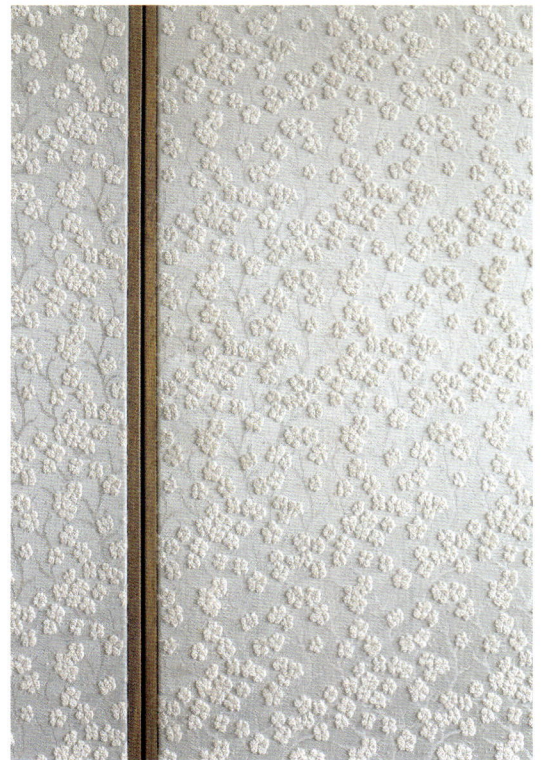

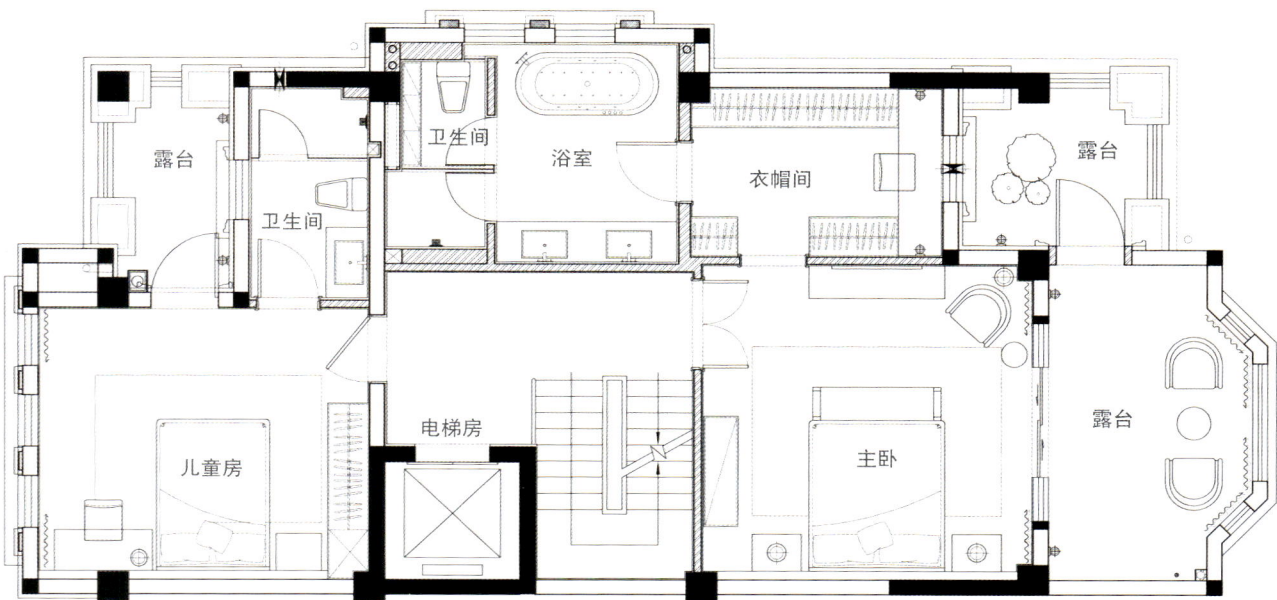

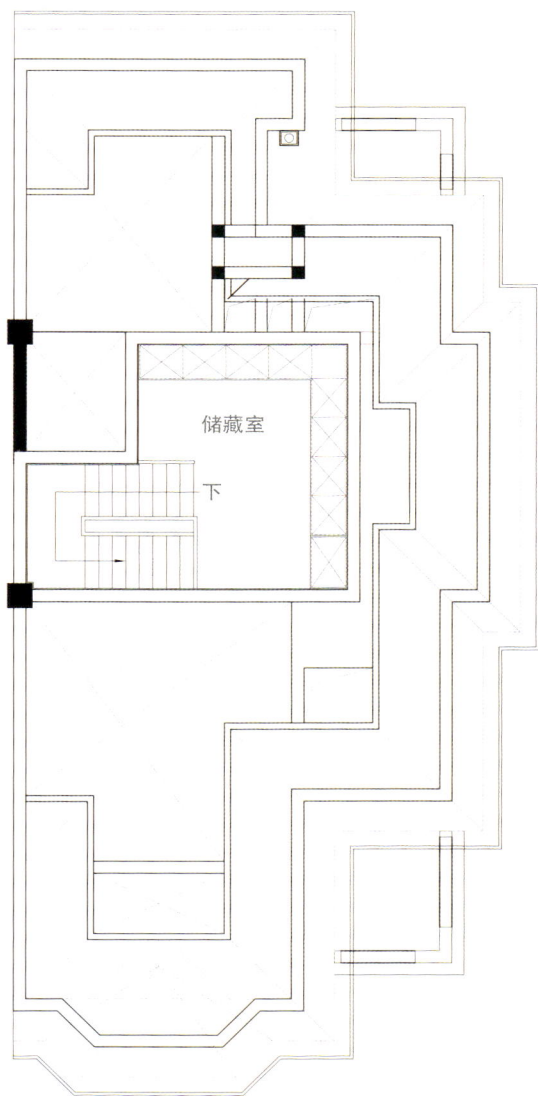

储藏室

下

二层作为长辈房与家庭娱乐区域，与整个空间的步调一脉相承。三层主卧是本套户型的最大亮点。卧室背景墙采用细木条竖向分割，简洁明朗的木质格栅、时尚稳重的家具以及暖色的灯光氛围，使空间兼具温馨舒适与典雅贵气。天花设计采用木架斜屋顶造型，大气而稳重；木质温润的触感、淡雅素净的配色及艺术品的点缀为主卧进行了全新的定位。露台设置品茶区域，挖掘生活情趣的更多可能性，饮茶赏景，投射出从容、自然的氛围。

在这座充满人文情怀的府邸里，生活的每一个细节，都可以感受到设计赋予生活更多的品质与意义，美感与功能共同成就了尊贵雅致的理想人居生活。

人文意蕴

摩登新中式的

THE HUMANISTIC CONNOTATION OF MODERN NEO-CHINESE STYLE

项目名称 | 郑州康桥悦蓉园新中式院墅

室内设计 | 戴勇室内设计师事务所（深圳）

陈设软装 | 深圳市布鲁盟设计有限公司

项目地点 | 河南郑州

项目面积 | 380 ㎡

主要材料 | 瓦尔赛金云石光面、米黄石、胡桃木饰面、胡桃木地板、地毯、布艺、皮革等

摄 影 师 | B+M Studio 赵宏飞

设计理念 | DESIGN CONCEPT

Kang Qiao Yue Rong Garden, as the plan of "neo-Chinese style villa" style, becomes the only new project of Chinese style residence in the entire region so far, with "careful design of architecture, and the reassuring service" to win the praise of market. The waterfront comes together with Eastern, and the Chinese aesthetics collides with the city reputation. The high rate of green coverage, the neo-Chinese style architecture and the Oriental artistic landscape appear stunningly.

This case integrates into the Oriental calmness and spirit, uses the traces of time to describe the gentleness and quietness, selects the modern Oriental language to create the elegant interest of modern culture, and discovers the humanistic meaning of this world which can not be replicated. This case selects the Chinese context combining with the local culture of Zhengzhou, and sublimates the neo-Chinese style with the modern design technique. The warm tone of whole house is quiet, soft and peaceful.

In the living room, a large area of walnut veneer and the classic maroon background wall complement each other, which highlight the nobility in simplicity. The fresh and natural white tea and the stable and tough ochre are like in the landscape and the artistic conception. The comfortable and gentle material with fabric texture and the stone tea table with exquisite and beautiful ornaments as embellishments make space in the simple, elegant and delicate conception extract a trace of modern temperament fitting with space, which is very suitable. The dining room continues to use a mature saddle brown color as basic color; the concise modern lines outline the calm and warm design of dining room; and the rich layers of metal geometry ceilings, marble dining table and wood dining chairs in dark red cloth allocating with novel white chandelier highlight a luxury atmosphere of the dining room.

　　康桥悦蓉园，以"新中式墅院"风格的规划，成为整个区域迄今为止唯一的新中式住宅项目，衡以"建筑匠心、服务安心"赢得市场赞誉。滨水与东方齐聚，中式美学与都会美誉碰撞。将以超高绿化率、新中式风格建筑、东方意境园林景观，惊艳登场。

　　项目融入东方沉稳灵性，用时光的痕迹细腻刻画温润与澄静，运用摩登东方语言营造当代人文高致，探寻这片天地不可复制的人文意蕴。本案用中式语境结合郑州当地文化以当代设计手法让新中式的格调得以再次升华，满屋温暖的色调平静人心而柔软温和。

　　客厅中，大面积胡桃木饰面与枣红色背景墙的古典相映得彰，质朴中彰显高贵。茶白的清新自然、赭石的稳重硬朗，犹如在山水之间，意境之中。布艺质感的材质舒适而温婉、石材茶几加以精巧绝美饰品的轻微点缀，让空间在质朴雅致的意境中又分外地提炼出一丝丝的当代气质与空间契合，不温不燥、不多不少、恰当刚好。餐厅依旧以成熟的马鞍棕为底色，精炼简洁的现代线条勾勒出沉稳温馨的餐厅设计，富有层次的金属几何线条天花、大理石餐桌与暗红布面实木餐椅，配合新颖的纯白吊灯，凸显出餐厅的奢华氛围。

When you go downstairs, video room and fitness area are at the entresol. The professional audio video equipment makes the owner have a luxurious private theater at home and the complete set of fitness equipment allows the owner to work and have a rest at home.

The basement two is mainly divided into four spaces, and the left is the wine cellar and art collection, the right is the study and tea tasting area. The whole space finds a transition and balance point in leisure, entertainment and works with the clear and flexible streamline. The walls of the calligraphy area and tea tasting room full of bookcases creating a calm spatial atmosphere, and a variety of art collections placed scatteringly, and all reflect the noble dignity of the host. The ultra-luxurious wine cellar with thermostatic wine cabinet, transparent wooden wine cabinet and bar fully meet the collecting and meeting needs of the owner.

The second floor of this villa is the master suite, the elder's room and children's room. The master room continues the whole color tone which is calm and elegant. The concise and powerful design language creates an elegant and comfortable artistic space full of artistic ingeniously. The concept of ink painting on the background wall is beautiful and meaningful, yet novel and unique, showing a quiet and elegant atmosphere perfectly. The fabric bed, the elegant and delicate maroon bedside cabinet with a ceramic vase and several strains of floral on it, allocating with two sandy lamps, all reveal a trace of romance in the classicism and reflect the warmth of home in grace. The private bedroom continues the elegance and peace of the whole space. All the spatial colors and forms reflect the evolution and blending of Oriental humanism.

拾级而下，夹层为影音室与健身区，专业的音画影视设备让主人在家就可以拥有豪华私人影院，配套齐全的健身设备则让主人在家也能劳逸结合。

负二层则主要划分出四大空间，左侧为酒窖和艺术品收藏区，右侧则为书房与品茶区，整个空间在休闲、娱乐和工作上找到了一个过渡与平衡点，流线清晰而灵活。书法区与品茶区满墙的书柜营造出沉稳的空间氛围，错落摆置着各种艺术藏品，无不反映主人的尊贵身份。超豪华酒窖内配有恒温红酒柜、实木造型通透红酒柜及吧台，完全满足业主的收藏与会客需求。

别墅的二层则为主人套间、长辈房和小孩房。主人房延续整体色调，沉静典雅，简洁有力的设计语言巧妙地营造优雅、舒适、富有艺术底蕴的艺术空间。背景墙水墨画意境清丽隽永，却新奇别致，完美地呈现静谧典雅的气质氛围，布艺的大床，雅致的枣红色床头柜，加上陶瓷花瓶和几株花艺，再配上两盏砂质的灯，在古典中透出一点小浪漫，在优雅中体现家的温馨。私密的卧室沿袭整个空间的清雅与平和，空间色彩之间、形式之内无一不在体现着东方人文的演变与糅合。

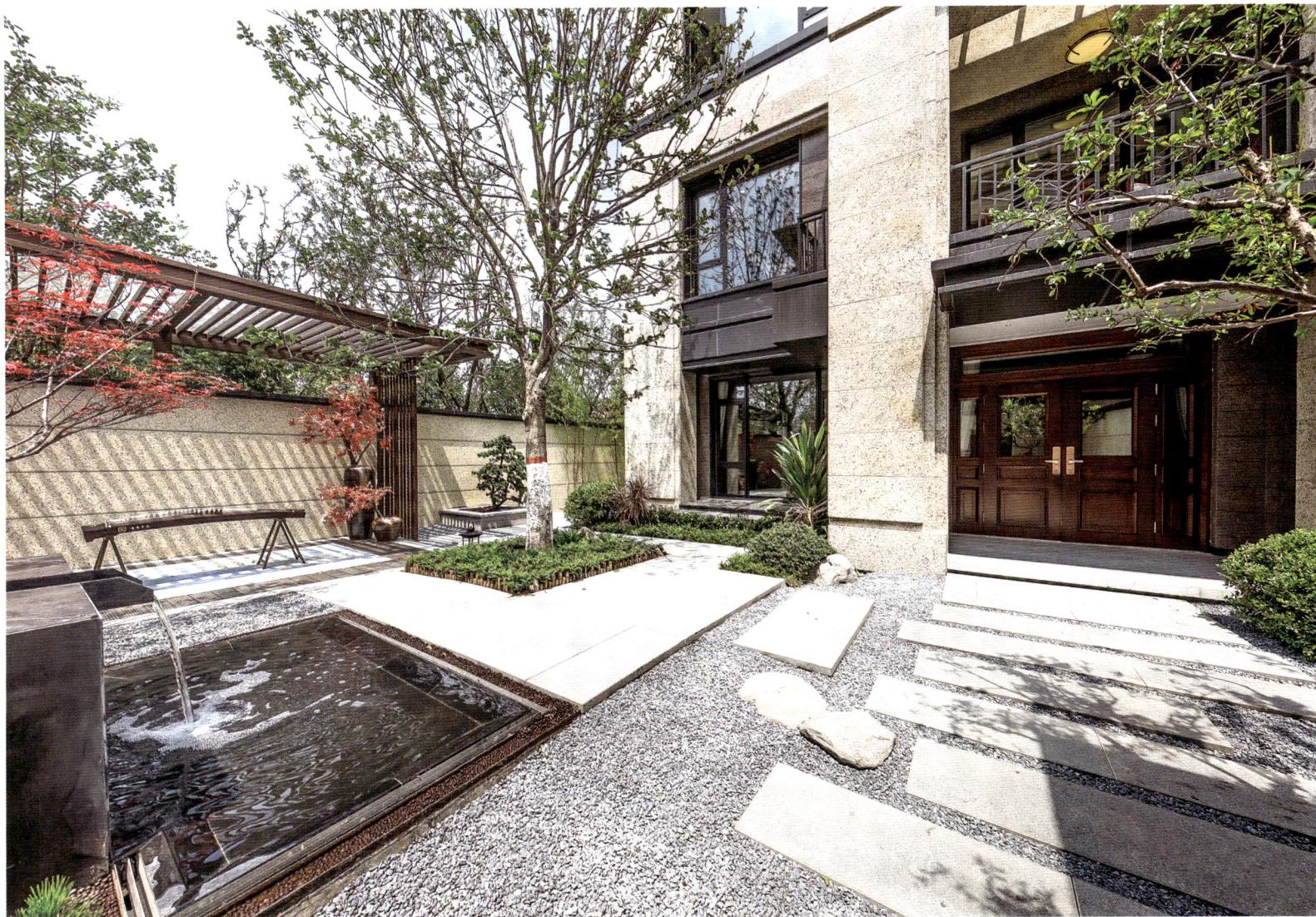

张清平

天坊室内计划
创始人、总设计师

Chang Ching -Ping

心奢华—Montage(蒙太奇)
美学风格

获得荣誉

出版个人著作《奢华》《龙的DNA》《清平调》

台湾室内设计业首位荣获德国红点设计大奖最高奖项"红
点金奖"(best of the best)

台湾唯一连续8次入选为英国安德马丁室内设计年度大奖
华人50强、全球100大顶尖设计师

英国安德马丁国际室内设计大奖

英国SBID国际设计大奖

德国红点设计大奖 Best of the Best

德国iF设计大奖

美国IDEA工业设计大奖

美国Interior Design "Hall of Fame名人堂"

美国IDA国际设计大奖

法国双面神国际设计大奖

意大利A'Design Award Competition等

设计自己的味道，创造美好生活

DESIGN YOUR STYLE, CREATE
A GOOD LIFE

视界对话张清平

张老师好，您作为台湾室内设计界首位获得红点奖金奖的设计师，对此项殊荣您最大的感受是什么？
您觉得什么样的设计才是好的设计？

张清平：身为设计工作者能获得德国红点奖室内设计的Best of the Best，我认为是在空间设计专业能
力上的认可。奖项是对于我个人在深度发掘文化与解读世界时尚能力上的重要肯定。

设计是什么？重点是"想别人所未想，做别人所未做"。好的设计，重点发掘关键性的关键，把它解决。

室内设计是什么？著名的雕塑《思考者》，我们说这个是藏在石头里面的灵魂。我们常说室内设计也不是一件商品，而是帮别人完成一个梦想。

您被台湾室内设计界誉为"台湾之光"，坚持让世界感受中国设计者的影响，在这个过程中您有什么心得和收获吗？

张清平：关于中国设计者的影响，我认为必须不遗余力向世界传达东方文化，这是一种使命。我的心得也是收获，就是能在喜欢的领域坚持我的创新与实践。用人的故事展现生活的轨迹，在历史的轨迹里面做中国人的设计，把我们的历史、文化底蕴里面的东西展现出来，这是一种虚无的意境，可能没有很多具象的对象植入，但能在空间中感受到这种气质。将这样的一种风格，同时也是生活的一种思维的中国式设计，让世界看到。

是您开创并一直坚持的蒙太奇美学风格吗？具体是什么？有哪些独特的艺术魅力？

张清平：Montage设计手法的解释就是减法与整合，并且以灵活的编辑手法来导演空间，通过分层与组接，对素材进行选择和取舍，以使空间内容主次分明，引导视觉进入焦点，激发张力的联想，创造出独特创意的空间。正如Montage让电影成为艺术，它也为空间设计带来时代感与美学价值。

以一个专业设计者的角度而言，我认为我们所设计的不是空间，而是生活。我们通过诗意现代化概念与现代空间的组构，为空间中的一道道美丽的人文景观导入中国人的文化底蕴，以空间蒙太奇的创新概念，剪接意境与实境，创造奢华态度与高度，让空间的使用者享受现代生活——这就是"心奢华"设计主张，这就是C.P. style。我们要设计出自己的味道，让世界来模仿。

不论空间的属性，从室内设计的整体规划，到美学装置的陈设，大量的运用我们记忆中熟悉的东方思想来结合西方建筑。也将西方流行的时尚元素，融入生活形态之中。以自己的美学意识去拆解，为空间使用者，进行转化与延伸，赋予更不一样更丰富的新内涵。塑造当代都会美学与时尚结合的生活形态。

Montage就是要揉合东西方故事的精华元素，将古今文化内涵完美地结合于一体，是一种向经典致敬的态度。充分利用空间形式与素材，整合古典、新古典、现代、东方、极简等各式风格，创造出个性化的家居环境。混搭只是把各种风格的元素放在一起做加法，而Montage是把故事元素以减法编辑。关键在于是否和谐，更结合现代与传统，并入多元文化，融合层次渲染效果的Montage，我认为是主流。

年轻人看了觉得很时尚，成熟的人看了觉得很怀旧，中国人觉得很西方，外国人则觉得很东方。是合璧也是华洋共处，是新旧交融同时也在怀旧的古典里，看见现代时尚。没有Montage，电影不能成为艺术。在空间设计的世界，没有Montage，将失去时代感与美学价值。

Montage内观且泰然，以无界为界。内观，是志学的方式，因而对生活吐纳宁静的智能；是聚德的工夫，因而对社会产生正面的贡献。泰然，是自恃的参透，依于仁的豁达；是综观的艺术，游于艺的优游人生。严谨、经典、坚固表现空间的洗炼精神。具体描绘居住者的品味及修为。彰显富而好礼、博施济众的品德，以及注重人文素养、虚怀若谷的气质。这就是Montage。

在您的简介里看到这句话，"坚持一个空间，不可能没有故事。"特别感动。对于设计来说，空间背后的故事是不是比设计本身更让人感动更有价值？

张清平：我想设计者都有一个重要的任务与价值：就是以设计专业，梳理出空间的故事，哪怕只是微小的细节。

我们可以用很多种方式找出它们之间的关系。设计需要加减乘除。加，是要加点想法，加点用心；减要减掉浮华；乘，要乘上细节，乘上质感；除，要除掉不实，除掉不智。以人为本，设计跟人不挂在一起，这个设计就没有意义了：人与人的关系，人与空间的关系，人与自己的关系。

您作为一位标签已经非常显著的设计名师，对于现在设计师树立自己品牌有什么看法和建议呢？

张清平：我一直认为身为设计师其实所设计的不仅仅是空间，而是生活方式。因此通过设计出积极阳光的生活态度来温暖空间的使用者。我相信一个成功的设计师，不论想树立的是怎样特色的品牌，在特质上一定是一个热爱生活、心态阳光，时时不忘初心的人，因此把美好的生活方式带给大家。

近年来台湾式设计在内地非常流行，非常受大众喜爱，可以跟我们谈谈对此的看法吗？

张清平：台湾历经许多年消费的价值观带动生活形态的改变之后，让人们越来越重视设计的情境性与内在的文化价值，同时凝聚许多设计者的努力，也因此催生了许多质感与动人的设计。我想这就是所谓台湾式的设计，有一种台湾式的特殊情怀。这些设计让人们可以跳脱出既有的框框，享受悠闲宁静与温暖的氛围。强调既见传统也见现代，既交融时尚又纳入简敛，既奢华贵气又自然朴质的交融各种趋向的独特性格，运用各种材质做对比，精心设计打造，细腻地传达体验式精神，达到实用又休闲的效果，创造精致有温度的生活美学。

这些经过沉淀温暖有故事性的设计在内地乃至国际上受到喜爱与重视，对于台湾出身的设计者而言，我认为是非常棒的，但于此同时我也感受到，设计者对于文化传承与优质生活营造的责任。

未来几年中国室内设计发展的趋势会有大的改变吗？

张清平：居民素质日益提高以及对环境的保护意识越来越强，所以有关绿色环保设计理念开始越来越受到人们的关注，绿色环保与节能技术开始日益在社会中得到迅速普及的发展，同时也会持续地成为室内设计发展的趋势。

跟您接触觉得您是一位特别谦卑、儒雅、温暖的老师，在设计中您也是这样的状态吗？生活中呢？

张清平： 其实我的设计状态就是我的生活态度。

我觉得设计，不只是设计空间或家具物品等，更能借着设计者的用心，将正向的、任何的对于自然、人文的美好的经验，可以超越限制，在人与人之间，人与空间的交流，创造微小而感动的美好关系。

最后可以跟我们谈谈如何才能够成为一名优秀并独立的设计师吗？

张清平： 成为优秀且独立的设计者的第一步 ——"做中学，学中做"，我认为这是必经之路！无论起点是什么，过程中都是一样的，勤于思考对流程作法深入的正确总结才能不断进步。

除了对于设计的热情，也要有拆掉思维里的墙的勇气，不断地给自己更大的思考空间。不断地重新认识自己，发掘潜力。当走过创意设计的阶段之后，就会向更高境界的设计研究方向发展，会开始自觉地去探索设计的根源，也在探索自己的风格与独物性。随着对设计的深层次理解与思考，自己的设计思维与设计领悟也会更上一个层次，以更宽的视野与更大的胸怀来做更好的设计。

张清平

Chang Ching -Ping

心奢华—Montage(蒙太奇)
美学风格

A PERFECT EXPERIENCE OF VISUAL CONNECTION

视觉联系的完美体验

设计公司 | 天坊室内计划
设 计 师 | 张清平
项目地点 | 四川成都
项目面积 | 309 ㎡
主要材料 | 大理石、水晶、不锈钢、皮革等

设计理念 | DESIGN CONCEPT

Taking the modern artistic villa design as concept, the designer not only creates a stylish residence for the elite circle but also creates a luxurious aesthetic villa with the theme of furnishing art and humanistic music.

The spatial design continues the consistent persistence, selecting the montage technique to tell the space story. The overall style is deeply influenced by the western aesthetics, and is also full of the historic elegance of Oriental culture. It is a contemporary aesthetic residence with the fusion of East and West. The smooth and graceful lines that run through all the layers of space are the modern western design language. By careful comparison, it is found that the cultural elements of the heyday of European and Eastern economies are simplified as the background. At the same time, through the dotted colors, it also evokes the vigor of The Arts and Crafts Movement and Art Nouveau in the 1840s and 1850s which are full of whimsy; then it uses the symmetry of Oriental grille, splash-ink rendering spatial color and other handling techniques which are the combinations of Chinese and Western to lead the Oriental humanistic spirit ingeniously; and integrates the Eastern and Western elements, music, strong lattice pattern, marble surface, calf and metal decorative lines into space gently and ingeniously. The handling of totem, colors and spatial lines is elegance-oriented and presents the line language rich in the sense ceremony in the low-key and restrained style which is in harmony with the contemporary design style. Creating its unique personality, every detail and every end scenery can exude a charm for people to enjoy a close distance.

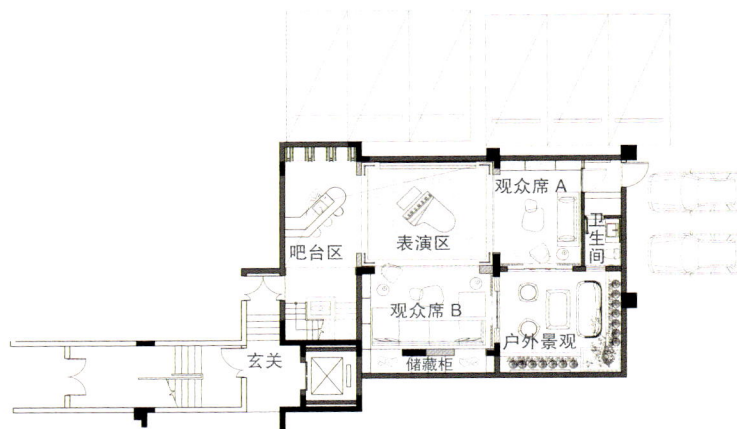

以设计现代艺术别墅为理念，同时为精英圈层打造时尚居处，更是创作出一座围绕着装置艺术与人文音乐为主题的美学豪墅。

空间设计遵循一贯的坚持，以蒙太奇手法来导演空间故事。整体的风格规划深受西方美学浸润影响，同时也充满东方人文的历史优雅，是融合东与西的当代美学住宅。贯穿于各层空间之中流畅优美的线条是理所当然的现代西方设计语言，仔细对比之下会发现室内蕴藏着欧洲和东方经济鼎盛时期的文化元素并将其简

化作为背景，同时也以点状的色彩唤起了充满奇想的40、50年代工艺运动、新艺术风格的神采；再以对称的东方隔栅、泼墨渲染式的空间色彩等东西合璧的处理手法巧妙地引出东方的人文精神；将东西方元素、音乐、强烈的格状图案、大理石表面、小牛皮和金属装饰线条等，细腻巧妙地融合到空间中，图腾、色彩与空间线条的处理，以优雅为主，低调内敛中呈现了富有形式感的线条语言，与当代设计风格共融互通，创造其独特的个性，每一处细节、每一个端景都能散发引人近距离去观赏的魅力。

Apart from the reasonable allocation of functional space and the open and the hidden pattern of life, the creation of this villa has the common ground in the application techniques of colors and patterns from the music room, painting room to the master suite. Adopting a design technique of a continuous rectangular space, one can enter into another space of different functions from one space unconsciously. At the same time, it strengthens the visual connection and continuity and makes space not only present a complete gorgeous temperament but also give people a feeling of being in a boutique art gallery. Life becomes a delicate and perfect experience. Echoing with the unique charm of the collision of new luxury and new Oriental, you can see a kind of new, modern and elegant lifestyle. At the same time, it also preserves the pursuit of literati which not only reveals a low-key luxury, but also integrates the humanity with architecture and the modernity with tradition to create the best comfort and maximum possibility of life.

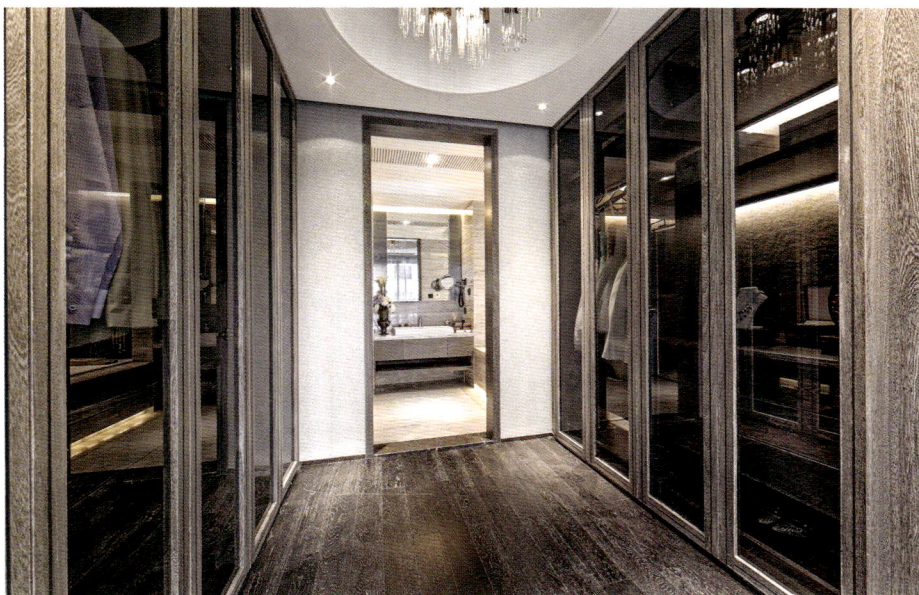

别墅的营造除了合理地分配功能空间与生活的开放与隐藏格局之外，更从音乐室、画室到主卧套间的色彩与图案的应用手法，都拥有着相互之间的共同点。通过采用一个连续的矩形空间设计手法，从一个空间不知不觉地就进入到另一个不同功能的空间，同时强化了视觉上的联系与延续，使得空间既呈现着完整的华丽气质，又给人一种置身于精品美术馆的感受，生活成为一场细致的完美体验。处处呼应新奢华与新东方所撞击出的独特韵味，可以见到一种新贵摩登而优雅的生活方式，同时也保存着文人追求，不仅流露出一种低调的奢华，而将人文与建筑、现代与传统融合，创造生活的最佳舒适性与最大可能性。

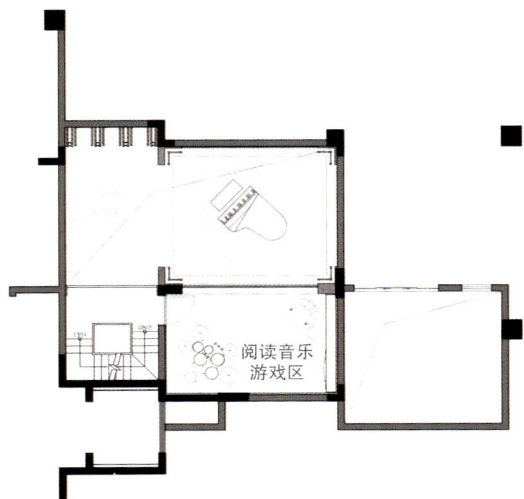

阅读音乐
游戏区

男孩房
书房
主卧
阳台
卫生间
楼厅
女孩房
主卫
衣帽间
下
上

葛亚曦

LSDCASA
创始人、艺术总监

Kot

立于潮流之外，艺术构建生活

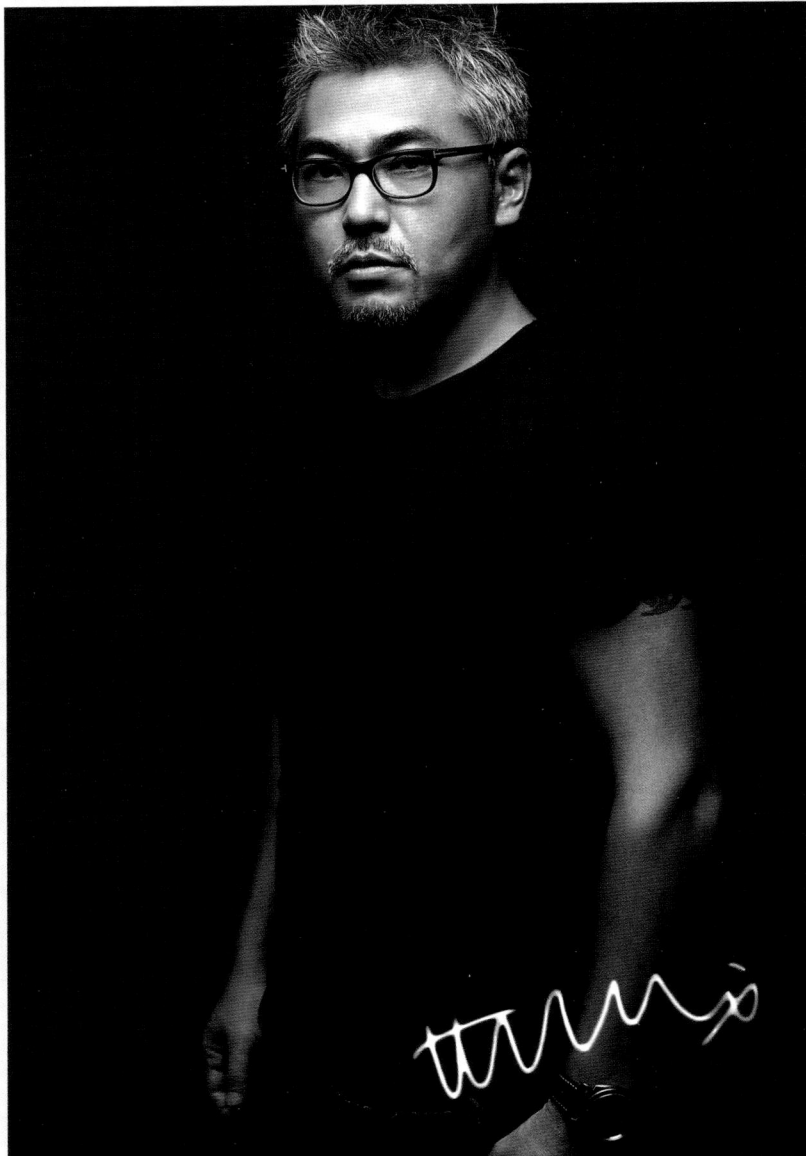

获得荣誉

2017年 意大利A'DESIGN AWARD&COMPETITION 室内设计与展示类银奖

2017年 地产设计大奖 中国（REDesign Award）室内类优秀奖

2017年 金外滩奖最佳居住空间单项大奖

2016年 APDC亚太室内设计精英赛2015-2016陈设金奖

2016年 入选英国ANDREW MARTIN国际室内设计大奖赛年鉴

2016年 中华室内设计2016年最具影响力设计机构奖

2016年 金堂奖年度样板房/售楼处空间最佳作品

2016年 美居奖最美别墅及最美样板间大奖

2016年 现代装饰国际传媒奖年度软装空间设计大奖

2015年 SBID国际设计大奖（英国）住宅类金奖等

学会审视自己，做个性有趣的设计

LEARNING TO EXAMINE OURSELVES, DOING A
PERSONALIZED AND INTERESTING DESIGN

视界对话葛亚曦

葛老师好，合作这么多年非常荣幸采访您，非常开心！因为会经常逛LSD的官方主页，里面有句话一直印象深刻，"你的家其实就是你"，可以给我们聊聊这句格言背后的含义吗？

葛亚曦：生活是一个人的品质外延，你是一个什么样的人，你的家就会呈现出什么样的气质，家的设计、家具的选择，其实包含了你的喜好、性格、生活的痕迹、态度，这是我们一直深信的。

您是从广告行业跨界到软装设计行业，并且在设计领域取得诸多成就与奖项，一路走来，在转行中有没有遇到一些特别深刻的事？

葛亚曦：我始终是一个设计师，我们都是创意产业，设计师的思考路径跟广告公司创意人的思考路径、思考系统是一样的，其实就是一个解决问题的方法和过程，它都需要你有理性探求真相的心和能力，以及敏锐的感受通道。在这点上，不管是平面设计、产品设计还是室内设计都是必须的。

室内设计对于我而言，其过程和我之前拍片子、拍视频是一样的，在于如何让我们所掌握的人的心理学、行为学、色彩感知等碎片化的知识，变成可以影响人与环境关系的因素。

前段时间我们去参加上海国际家居展，在展会上看到您的家居品牌"再造"场面火爆，当初您创立"再造"这个品牌的初衷和目的是什么？

葛亚曦：我们一直觉得我们所面对的环境比较不堪或有待改善，一直在为改变这件事而努力，让我们生活在友善、礼貌、相信自己、保持情趣的环境里。这是我们10年前创立公司的愿景和初衷，也仍然是我们"再造"的原点。

现在很多设计师主张"轻硬装，重软装"，作为软装设计师您对此有什么看法？未来室内设计的趋势会不会有所改变？

葛亚曦：轻硬装，重软装——我理解的这句话里的"轻"与"重"，指的是装饰程度，而不是重视程度。

本质上硬装是对软装设计的前提，约束风格范围，形成限制。过去十几年，大家装修都是拼命地堆砌各种装饰元素，各种风格标签，电视墙要豪华，吊顶得吊三层，然后可能现在大家开始慢慢意识到自己的品位需要被伸张，自己的风格需要被体现，"家"需要随着主人对美、对趣味

的认知成长改变而包容或改变，而太多的约束就会限制这种可能。

未来随着消费成熟，大家对个性化的需求越大，这种做法会越来越多。

LSDCASA从创立至今一直坚持"立于潮流之外，艺术构建生活"的设计理念，在设计中您是如何做到平衡商业诉求和艺术创意之间的关系？

葛亚曦：我们一直把艺术价值作为衡量我们设计好坏的重要指标，关注设计工作对人的品性、趣味、生活的构建。艺术的"美"是个动态的存在，没有方法论，而商业的诉求需要有清晰的目标和路径去接近。基于这两点，我们在设计中坚持以情操、价值观作为内核，形式美作为外形的理论认知体系来提供参照，就有了平衡的路径。

有趣作为现在非常流行的一个词，您觉得设计有趣的点在哪里？

葛亚曦：设计这个工作和其他创作活动一样，永远有更好的解决方案，决定了它的趣味和魅力，诱使着你不断地发现和坚持，我觉得这是我们最大的动力。

最后，想听听您对未来年轻一代设计师们有些什么感想或者期望？

葛亚曦：设计师必须要有训练自己思维的能力，其次在艺术修养、某些个性上面，比如要有自检的能力来克服自己的自恋，千万不要太过相信和迷恋你自己现在的看法和判断，但也不是因此去怀疑自己，而是激励自己去寻找更好的答案。

设计工作的本身并不是去表达自我，所以对于某一些设计师而言这件事情就不是成本。一个案子里面要让设计师消失，这是我认为一个设计师应该做的事儿。

大道无形 和光同尘

INTERPRETING THE MANSION WITH INVISIBLE TAO THOUGHT

项目名称 | 保利·和光尘樾

建筑设计 | 筑博设计

景观设计 | 奥雅设计

硬装设计 | 邱德光设计事务所

软装设计 | LSDCASA

项目地点 | 北京

设计理念 | DESIGN CONCEPT

Blunt the sharp and solve the dispute; soften the light and mingle with dust so as to be one with the mysterious law.

——Lao Zi, *Tao Te Ching · The Fifty and Six Chapter*

What Lao Zi said is the real "Tao", which is living with the custom like the light and dust.

We date from the fragment of Chinese and Western aesthetics which is the nature and casual of Wei and Jin Dynasties, the pursuit of "clumsiness", "innocent", and "ordinary" of literati's tastes in North Song Dynasty, or the ultimate Japanese "Wabi-Sabi". It is easy to find that the process of exploring beauty should experience the process of blunting the sharp and solving the dispute and finally softening the light and mingling with dust. Picasso once said, " I can draw as well as Rafael at 14, and then I spend my whole life learning how to paint like a child."

But this doesn't be proved in today's Chinese architecture and residential culture. Our life will always be caught up by one and one fashionable trend, covered by one and one doctrine, and the chase of representation and form seems never to end. While the cognitive of wealth flows and constantly relays between different labels, from Rome column to marble mosaic, Ming style chairs, calligraphy and painting, or beads. What is more puzzling is the obsessiveness and the self-righteous interpretation of the so-called "design sense".

Beijing Poly Heguangchenyue decides to create an architecture which can bear life yet not paste the style in the concept of the luxury market, and lets us see the concern of Poly development and design team for the city and the promotion of aesthetic thinking.

挫其锐，解其纷；和其光，同其尘；是谓玄同。

——老子《道德经·第五十六章》

老子说的是真正的"道"，是随俗而处，如光如尘。

我们追溯中外美学的吉光片羽——无论是魏晋时期"初发芙蓉胜过缕金错彩"的自然随性，还是北宋时追求"拙""天真""平淡"的文人品味，或者被奉为极致的日本"侘寂"，不难发现——对美的求索里程，有一个挫其锐，解其纷，而最终和光同尘的过程。毕加索也曾说，"我14岁就能画得像拉斐尔一样好，之后我用一生去学习如何像小孩那样画画。"

但这件事在如今中国的建筑和居住文化中，似乎不被验证。我们的生活总是被一个又一个潮流追赶，被一个又一个主义覆盖，对表象和形式的追逐好像永远没有尽头，而对财富的认知则不断流转接力于不同的标签之间，从罗马柱到大理石拼花，再到明椅、字画或串珠。更不解的是，对不知所谓的所谓"设计感"的执念和自以为是的演绎。主线提升空间的端庄、仪式感，餐厅引入自然园林对景，以八角形形成空间的围合感，传达和谐的幸福之美.

北京保利和光尘樾在堆满概念的豪宅市场，决意打造一个用以承载生活而非粘贴风格的建筑，让我们看到保利开发及设计团队对城市的关怀和对推进审美的思考。

And LSD insists that the design comes from solving problems. This is the most basic value of design. Based on the premise of solving the problem, the designer expressed selectively to establish the emotional relation and distinction, so that the style is changed. After these two situations, the design which reflects a reflection and outputs the value of times determines whether it is noble or vulgar. Anything catering to the market is essential to tribute wealth, which will eventually be iterated, even with a mask of poetry or art.

The building is a five-storey villa, and the atrium lighting patio is a vertical lighting center throughout the residence. The basement one and two are planned to the space accommodating the owner's hobbies. The first floor is the living space with front and rear courtyard, which is the most precious building resources. The second and third floors are the space for the family to live.

The design is always a process of selection, and each "taking" and "abandoning" is related to the understanding of function, the modulation of value and the sense of beauty. While we are also in the process of this choice, gradually form a style and a temperament.

Lighting Atrium

The most distinguishing feature of this building is the 17-meter-tall lighting atrium through the five floors which is the most important core area for creating the memory point of "light". The first instinct of the designer was to leave the blank and tried to decorate this space with seasonal themes or more artistic, expressive forms. While when the designer stood at the bottom of the courtyard again, there were two lights on the wall, moving and weaving slowly in the afternoon until the warm red sunset filled the glass box. So the designer began to confirm that the light changing with the time and weather is the best and the only decoration for this space.

The Living Room and Dining Room On the First Floor

What needs to be solved in the design is rationalizing the space and creating resources on the base of the building. As the living space in this house, the first floor is the first part for us to recognize this house. An interval of indoor garden forms a psychological feeling on the outdoor entrance. After entering a space into the living room, it can maximize the wide vision of living space to match building scale. Integrating the two courtyards of the North and South as the extension of the living function, the design of courtyard is developed for indoors, and considered as a whole with living room and dining room in layout.

而LSD坚持，设计因解决问题而生，这是设计最基础也是最根本的价值所在。基于解决问题的前提，选择性地表达，以此建立情感联系、建立区别，也就发生了风格。而在这二者之后，设计对时代发出的反思、所输出的价值观，决定了它是高贵还是凡俗。任何迎合市场的做法，本质上是致敬财富，终究会被迭代，即便戴着诗意或艺术的面具。

建筑为五层别墅，中庭采光天井，是垂直贯穿整个居所的采光中心。地下两层规划为容纳主人性格喜好的空间，一层起居空间拥有前后庭院，是建筑最珍贵的资源，二、三层则是家人居住的空间。

设计永远是一个选择的过程，每一次的"取"与"舍"都关乎对功能的理解、价值的抑扬和对美的感知。而我们也在这种选择的过程中，逐步形成风格，气质。

采光中庭

这个建筑的最大特征是贯穿于5层空间17米高的采光天井，这里是营造"光"记忆点最重要的核心区域。设计师的第一直觉是留白，也曾尝试过以季节变化的主题，或更加艺术化的表现形式来装点这个空间，但当设计师又一次站在那个天井的底部，有两道光打在墙面，并在午后慢慢地移动、交织，直到暖红色的夕阳灌满这个玻璃盒子……于是设计师开始坚定，光随着时间、天气而流转的变化，将是这个空间最好、并且唯一的装饰。

一层客餐厅

让空间合理化并在原建筑基础创造资源是设计需要解决的问题。一层作为这个居所的起居空间，也是我们认识这个家的第一步。间隔入户花园，形成心理感受上的户外玄关，入户后空间纳入客厅整体，让客厅的面宽视觉最大化，以此匹配建筑的尺度。整合南北两个庭院作为起居功能的延伸，庭院的设计向室内发展，布局上与客餐厅视为整体考虑。

In the layout, the designer used the main sofa and big tea table to create a stable surface, producing primary and secondary relations and spatial rhythm. In the selection of furniture, restraining the desire of deduction and egocentricity gives way to architecture and space.

The unique tea table was made personally by the French artist, three color bricks on the table can be traced back to the 50-60 era of last century, and the antique armchair aside also had the sign of Corbusier. The design of that era began to turn to be functional without any unnecessary decoration. All lines must be restraint and necessary.

Every arrangement has its own story yet not ostentatious, and not afraid of being discovered and ignored. This is the source of this space full of proud power.

Basement Two

Architecture or hard decoration is the premise and limitation of soft decoration design, but all innovations start with limitations. Our work is making the original design intent more explicit because of our intervention. Most of the time, we need to dismantle some seemingly reasonable irrationality, and defuse the interference.

The biggest core of the basement two is a huge LED screen with a height of 7 meters and a width of 9 meters. Based on the comfort degree of visual experience and the principle of the design target which is designing the model room for private interest, the designer removed the darkroom, combined with the bearing columns to form a high bar, opened the original closed space, and connected with the multi-functional long table on the right side to create a space for tea tasting, cigars and wine tasting. The space is greatly extended and accommodates a variety of social interactions.

The designer rearranged the layout and volume of the furniture in this space. When the video screen is used, people can get the best visual effect at the most comfortable distance. While it is not used, the arrangement of enclosed furniture also can make people have a chat or hold a party in this space, which is intimate.

Basement One

As the hostess' space, the essential goal of the design is to strengthen the interaction in the usage between the basement one and basement two. In the original plan, the stability and ethereal attributes of yoga room conflict in the open interactive space, and the design of video room and cloakroom is ambiguous. Thus, the designer added the handmade desk, gym and study to make the matching of space and function more reasonable, and also used more 3D stereo scenes to show the personalities, careers and hobbies of the characters.

In the initial stage of the design, this building left a sunshine shared with basement one and basement two. The trajectory and angle of light are carefully measured, so that when the designer moved the fitness equipment in front of the high-empty glass on basement one, people can feel a sense of outdoor gym in this underground fitness room.

The Parent-child Activity Area, Children Room and the Elder's Room the Second Floor

The second floor has three personalized living spaces connected by parent-child area, which the core goal is to make the intent and skill of design give way to life.

The elder's room is nature and comfortable, using the matte finish and handmade texture; the color tone of girl's room is peaceful and gentle, full of girlish sensation, interweaving with the suitable decorations which echo the origami theme of space; while with the theme of space adventures, the boy's room integrates the wallpaper, bedding and carpet into the whole space, creating dreams for the little boy who loves space and is full of curiosity and imagination.

The Master Bedroom and Study On the Third Floor

The designer integrated the original locker room with the cloakroom behind the background wall of the master bedroom, which can broaden 900mm width of the master bedroom and master bathroom, letting those unnecessary functions give way to the space experience and necessary scale.

Each design should have its language and grammar to form the concept, embodying in the choice of every color and the touch of every material. Weakening the concept of background wall instead of a calm and introverted solid color, echoing with the dark blue velvet in the bed from Italy ceccotti, people can have a comfortable sleep here.

The designer selected the square artist unique desk fitting with the stable needs of space as a semi-open study, and used the handmade metal and leather showing a warm temperament, which together with the artwork and sculpture on the bookshelves can constitute the main character of this space.

在布局上，用主沙发和大茶几来创造稳定面，产生主次关系和空间节奏。在家具选择上，克制演绎和自我中心的欲望，让位于建筑和空间。

法国艺术家亲手打造的孤品茶几，台面上的三块彩砖可以追溯到20世纪50~60年代，一旁的古董单椅亦可窥探到柯布西耶的影子。那个时代的设计开始转向功能化，卸除不必要的装饰，所有线条克制而必须。

每一个安排都有自己的故事，却不招摇，不害怕不被发现和忽略，正是空间充满骄傲的力量来源。

负二层

建筑或硬装是软装设计开始的前提，也是限制，但所有的创新都由限制开始，我们的工作，是让原来的设计意图因我们的介入而更加明确，更多时候，我们需要去拆解一些看似合理的不合理，化解干扰。

负二层最大的核心是高7米宽9米的巨幅LED屏，基于视觉观看舒适度的考量，以及不以私趣为样板房设计目标的原则，设计师拆去暗房，结合承重柱，形成半高水吧台，开放原封闭空间，与右侧的多功能长桌，共同构建了一个复合了茶室、雪茄、品酒的空间，使空间大幅延展，并能容纳更多样的社交。

重新排布了空间的家具布局和体量。让影音屏在使用时，能够以一个最舒适的距离得到最佳的视觉效果；而在不使用影音屏时，围合相洽的家具排布也能让这个空间的交谈、聚会，亲密"有间"。

负一层

作为女主人空间，设计的本质目标在于加强负二层与负一层感受和使用上的互动，原规划中，瑜伽房的稳定、空灵的属性冲突于开放性交互空间，影音室与衣帽间的设计，面目含糊。于是，设计师加载了手作台、健身房和书房，让空间与功能的匹配趋于合理，并用更多元立体的场景将人物的个性、事业、爱好呈现出来。

建筑在设计的初始阶段，为此空间留下一抹由负二、负一共享的阳光，光的轨迹和角度都经过精心测量，当设计师将健身器材搬到负一层的挑空玻璃前，这个在地下的健身室，也能有一种户外健身房的感观。

二层亲子活动区、儿童房、老人房

住宅二层，以亲子活动区连接起3个秉性各异的居所。核心目标是让设计的意图与手法让位于生活。

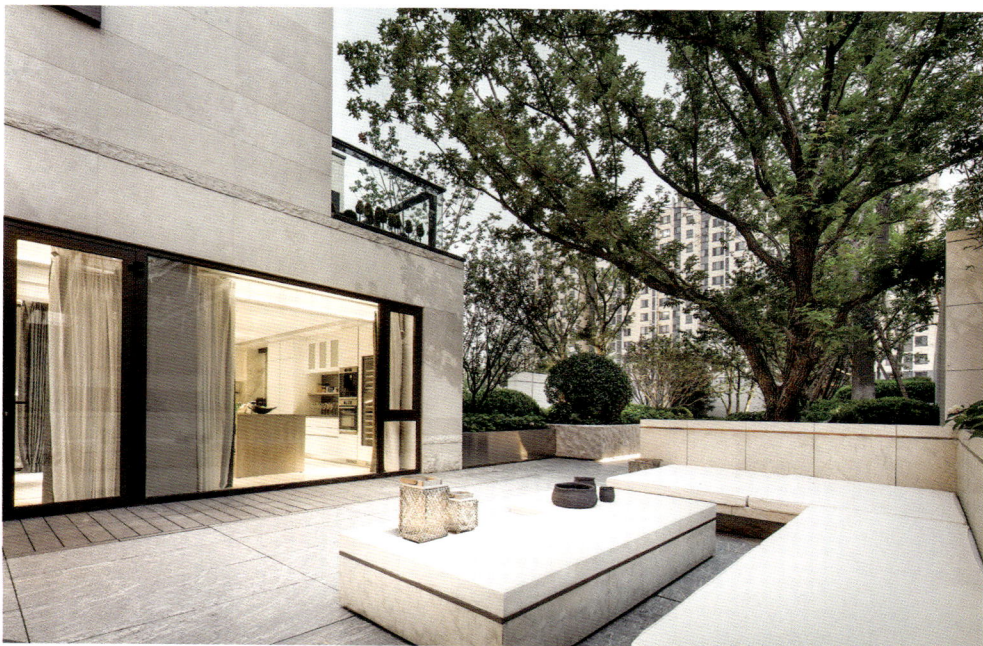

老人房以自然舒适为要义，多采用哑光饰面和手工质感的肌理；女孩房色调舒缓温和，少女感十足，恰到好处的饰品轻柔交织，契合空间折纸主题；男孩房则以太空探险为主题，从墙纸、床品到地毯的选择融合在空间之中，为这个热爱太空充满好奇心和想象力的小男孩营造梦境。

三层主卧、书房

设计师将原更衣室整合到主卧背景墙后的衣帽间，为主卧和主卫的面宽分别拓宽900mm，让那些非必须的功能让位于空间体验感和必要的尺度。

每一个设计要有自己的语言和语法来形成语境，体现在每一个颜色的选择，每一款材质的触感之中。弱化背景墙概念，以沉稳内敛的纯色替代，与来自意大利ceccotti的床深蓝绒布相呼应，安放每一个舒适的睡眠。

选择了方形的艺术家孤品书桌，契合作为半开放书房的空间稳定需要，用手工锻打的金属和皮质给人以温暖的气质，与书柜上的艺术品和雕塑一起，构成了这个空间的主要个性。

PUTTING HUMANITY INTO DESIGN

把温度写入设计

项目名称 | 北京金茂府

硬装设计 | 朱周空间设计

软装设计 | LSDCASA

项目地点 | 北京

项目面积 | 470 ㎡

设计理念 | DESIGN CONCEPT

Nowadays, we go to any city what it wants to show us is almost in common -- the grotesque "iconic" buildings, dazzling glass curtain walls. While the so-called local personality is broken down into the residual forms and concepts which are made of cheap materials and advertised to defraud visitors come in a throng.

In the globalizing China, the strong culture influences us all the time, and the similar cultural environment and trend steal our memories and humanities of a city and change our architectures, designs and ideologies.

Beijing Jin Maofu is located in the south of Temple of Heaven. The developer hoped that the existing of this project could build an urban life function, urban reconstruction and updated new sample. It requires our design to carry some city's memories but can not linger in the past.

Facing the local and modernness is the starting point of our design. For the living concepts of urban memories like old Hutong and Siheyuan, we extracted its spiritual appeals like the order of family ethics and the temperature of human integrating into the modern living environment and spatial pattern straight to the heart from the emotional level without forms.

我们今天去到任何一个城市，它愿意展示给我们的那一面，几乎都是千篇一律的——奇形怪状的"标志性"建筑，争相耀眼的玻璃幕墙，而所谓地方个性被拆解成残留的形式和概念，用廉价的材料高高挂起，骗取纷至沓来的游客到此一游。

在这个被全球化车轮裹挟着滚滚向前的中国，强势文明在无时不刻地影响我们，趋同的文化环境和潮流，挟持了城市记忆和温度，改变着我们的建筑、设计和意识形态。

北京金茂府地处天坛正南，开发商希望这个项目的出现，能够构建城市生活机能体及城市修复、更新的崭新样本。这就需要我们的设计去承载一些城市的记忆，而又不能流连于过去。

直面本土，直面现代——这是我们设计的出发点。对于城市记忆的居住观念，如老胡同和四合院，我们提取它的精神诉求，比如家庭伦理的次序和人情的温度，结合到现代居住环境和空间格局之中，离开形式，从情感层面直切内心。

The design of living room prefers the comfortable functions, openness and brightness. A large area space with gray and white color as a basis, mixing with the color collocation of green and orange color contrast, and the furniture echoing the concise space whose lines are also directly and simply without any unnecessary decorations, all of these seemly casual collocations are naturally. The chandelier in mountain-shaped elements gives the dining room a unique temperament, and the placement of tableware adopting a more artistic form to echo with overall living style. In the selection of accessories, the implantation of withered landscape and other elements, which is combined with strong modern sense and oriental aesthetics, represents the harmony and unit of quality and art.

The texture and style of a home maybe begin from the location. Whether it is space, furniture, arts, or Feng Shui, the charm and the owner's lifestyle, the texture of a house needs every choice, every action, and even every emotion to create together.

The master bedroom is a private and relaxing place for the owner. The gray color with dark or light layers and the bumpy texture of fabric are introduced from outside to inside, and the interspersed orange color makes the vocabulary of interior devices and materials create a simple, pure and comfortable dialogue.

The boy's room with the theme of "ice hockey" and the playful collocation of blue and red fully represents a lively and happy personality of a boy. The girl's room is used a soft tone of pink and green as a basis. The soft and comfortable curtains full of girlish sensation, interspersing the suitable accessories gently create a warm dream that is unwilling to wake up.

Basement one and basement two are the common places for every

family member to create happy memories. The fitness area is facing the French glass windows. From it, one can see a whole ecological wall and feel relaxing. The yoga room receives the first ray of sunshine in the morning everyday. It is also a place to avoid the complexity, quarrel and noise, and comfort one's heart.

It is worth mentioning that the basement one is connected with the basement two through a childlike slide to build a fun paradise for children. Not far away, the rock climbing wall is designed to move the children's activity space from the ground to the wall ingeniously, which can save space. In such a functional layout, it can provide more interactions for children and parents.

In order to continue the concept of "courtyard" and produce "landscape" into indoors, we make the design give way to natural light. The natural light is introduced by transparent patio echoing with the vertical height-raised ecological rain forest wall, showing a leisure and comfortable feeling.

　　客厅设计更加偏向舒适的功能性，开阔明亮，大面积以灰白打底，混合绿色和橘色对比的色彩搭配，家具款式呼应空间的简洁，线条亦十分直接、干脆，似乎没有一丝多余，看似不经意的搭配之下，一切浑然天成。山形元素的吊灯赋予了餐厅别样的气质，餐具的摆放，采用更加艺术化的形式，呼应整个居所的格调。饰品选择上，植入枯山水等元素、极强的现代感与东方美学结合，呈现出品质与艺术的和谐统一。

　　一个家的质地与风情，或许从选址时就已经开始，不论是空间、家具、艺术品，还是风水、气韵和主人的生活方式，一个家的质感，需要每一个选择、每一次动作，甚至每一份情绪来共同编织。

主卧室是主人私密与尽情放松的地方，以或深或浅层次的灰色及凹凸质感的布艺自外而内导入，恰到好处点缀的橘色，令室内装置与材质建构的语汇之间，产生一种与简单、纯粹、舒适共鸣的对话形式。

男孩房以"冰球"作为空间的主题，蓝色和红色颜色的俏皮搭配，充分把这个大男孩跳脱快乐的性格表现出来。女孩房则以粉绿色的柔美基调打底，轻柔舒适的窗帘，少女感十足，恰到好处的饰品轻柔地点拨，营造一个不愿醒来的温馨美梦。

负一层、负二层是每个家庭成员制造快乐记忆的共同场所，健身区面对着落地玻璃窗，可以看到一整面生态墙、让人放松。瑜伽室则在每天迎来清晨的第一缕阳光，这里也是避开复杂、争吵和喧嚣的世外桃源，让心得到慰藉的地方。

最值得一提的是，负一层通过一个充满童趣的滑梯与负二层相连，为孩子们构建了一个玩乐的天堂。不远处则是以攀岩墙的设计，将孩子的活动空间从地上巧妙地挪到墙上，节省了空间。在这样的功能布局上，孩子和家长有了更高的互动性。

为了延续"院"的概念并把"景"影射进室内，我们把设计让位于自然光，通透的天井将自然光顺势带下，又有垂直挑高生态雨林墙与之呼应，临摹出一派闲适自在。

创始人、设计总监

SCD（香港）郑树芬设计事务所

郑树芬

Simon Chong

"雅奢主张"开创者

获得荣誉

出版作品集《居室韵律》《构》《雅奢主张》

2016年 SCD（香港）郑树芬设计事务所荣获"中国室内设计二十年总评榜最具创新设计机构"

2016年 郑树芬先生荣获"中国室内设计行业杰出贡献"奖

2016年 郑树芬先生荣获年度优秀别墅设计金堂奖

2016年 郑树芬先生、杜恒女士荣获年度优秀别墅设计金堂奖

2015年 SCD香港郑树芬设计事务所荣获第十届金盘奖·西南西北赛区年度最佳预售楼盘奖

2015年 SCD香港郑树芬设计事务所荣获第十届金盘奖·华南赛区年度最佳样板房奖及媒体推荐奖

2015年 郑树芬先生、杜恒女士荣获"2015年BEST100中国最佳设计"奖

2015年 郑树芬先生荣获中国室内设计行业年度评选"最具国际影响力设计师奖"等

空杯心态，快乐有趣地做设计
EMPTY YOUR ACHIEVEMENTS, DESIGN HAPPILY AND INTERESTINGLY

视界对话郑树芬

郑老师好，作为开创者，可以跟我们分享一下您的"雅奢主张"吗？具体是什么？

郑树芬：我认为雅奢主张是将低调奢华的气质"自然而不着痕迹地融入当地文化"的设计理念，以展现当代内敛奢华的气度，注重空间的人文特质正是"雅奢"重要的表达方式之一。

在空间中，您是通过哪些方式诠释"雅奢主张"的？

郑树芬：每个项目除了对建筑及室内情况的了解，还要结合客户对空间设计的期望及要求，表达风格的同时还需要从材料、家具及艺术品的选择多方融入去诠释空间想表达的意境。

现在越来越多年轻人喜爱上"雅奢"这个词，淡淡地复古与时尚。跟您合作出版这么多年，每次您的作品我们都能从中读出与众不同的历史韵味，无论是古典风格还是现代风格，您都能做出您自己的味道，您是怎么做到的呢？

郑树芬：哈哈（笑）谢谢！其实我也没有特意地去做与众不同，闲暇时会去世界各地看不同的设计发现有趣新颖的材料，还会参观很多艺术品展，希望通过接收更多好玩有趣的东西将它们有机会放在项目里，这样就可能呈现每个项目设计的多变性了。

我们都知道您是非专业出身，能有现在的成就与地位，一定付出了很多心血，当初是抱着怎样的信念要坚持做设计的呢？

郑树芬：因为喜欢、爱好。设计一直是我很喜欢做的事情，当物质财富积累到一定程度之后，我们的内心总会有着更高的追求。当时接触的银行VVIP客户都是社会名流，通过给他们设计豪宅发现设计带给我的快乐更加美好，而且长期的经验积累，让我的客户也源源不断，所以一直坚持做下去了。

您觉得作为一名好的设计师最重要的是什么？

郑树芬：我觉得最重要的是自己的内心，如果做的事情是由衷的发自内心喜欢的，我相信一定能去做好它。

在设计中，如何平衡好设计效果与客户需求之间的冲突？

郑树芬：很幸运的是目前大部分的客户对我都是非常信任的，当然如果遇到有意见不一致的客户时，首先我还是会从专业的角度去分析讲解给对方听，相信只要是合理的对项目好的，客户也一定能够理解的。

一个好的设计项目，最需要具备的有哪些？

郑树芬：我觉得客户的信任很重要，其次是沟通，相信所有的问题都可以通过良好及密切的沟通去解决的。

对于您自己的设计项目，目前为止，您最满意的是哪个？为什么？

郑树芬：二十几年来设计了很多很多的项目，每一个对我来说都是很用心去做出来的，每一个都很满意，只是每个项目除了从专业角度还要结合客户对项目设计要求去看的时候，大家的理解不同而已。

从您设计的项目中能看到很多艺术品、收藏品用于装饰，是您个人爱好吗？做设计项目的时候如何正确的挑选装饰品提升空间品质？

郑树芬：是的，我最大的兴趣爱好就是去发现和收藏极具代表且具有升值潜力的艺术品。至于每个项目在艺术品方面的选择很大程度上还是要根据项目本身的定位以及风格表现的需要去做选择，当然也要结合客户的喜欢以及在这方面投入的预算去考虑。

对于年轻设计师，如何更有效更快速的提高自己审美与艺术修养，可以给一些建议吗？

郑树芬：我觉得人一生应该活到老学到老，不断地去接收新的讯息并理解消化它，这也是不断提升自我的唯一途径。

如果要您用一句话总结您的设计生活，是什么？背后有什么深刻含义吗？

郑树芬：我可以用两个词来总结吗？哈哈（笑）！我觉得我的设计生活用快乐和有趣两个词就可以总结了，设计是自己喜欢做的事情，而且可以从中找到很多乐趣，这样的生活已经很有意义了。

除了设计，在生活中您是什么样子的？平时会做些什么？

郑树芬：平时生活中工作之余会逛艺术画廊，收藏挂画艺术品，跟朋友聚会，外出旅行……这些方式能让我很好地放松，又可以从中获得灵感反馈到设计中。

文人大宅的礼赞

A PAEAN FOR A LITERATI MANSION

项目名称 | 海航·豪庭北苑

设计公司 | SCD（香港）郑树芬设计事务所

主案设计师 | 郑树芬、徐圣凯

软装设计师 | 杜恒、丁静

项目地点 | 海南海口

项目面积 | 417 ㎡

主要材料 | 索罗门米黄地台、瑞典橡木地板、墙纸、大理石、仿古铜板等

设计理念 | DESIGN CONCEPT

Because of beauty, we can keep moving on.

-- Jiang Xun

In this space covering 417 square meters, we tried to have a dialogue with ancient and modern times, looked for a beauty of balance, and represented our understanding and pursuit of beauty in this space. Zhuang Zi had said, "Nature has its great beauty, yet does not speak of it.", and he thought that all nature not concerning about the advantages and disadvantages and the gain and loss, and confirming the unity of rules and intentions, that is the great beauty. But all beauties and all arts are eventually embodied in human beings. So when you touch a leaf, taste a cup of tea, listen to the wind through the forest, you can feel the beauty and find the meaning of moving on.

Suddenly, it snows all the night which is the first surprise in the morning. The princes enjoy the snow on the pavilion or play the ice on the lake; the children play in the snow and the servant girls are busy to clean up the snow on the corridor. All the scenes are beautiful, and as if we can hearing the laughter. What is a beautiful story performing on the prosperous Old Summer Palace in that year?

The elegant and delicate Chinese style screen allocating with tough European lines, the highly textured dining table and chairs and the silk carpet make the ceremonial sense of the whole dining room relaxed and comfortable. Listening to the wind, tasting the tea, round moon, wintersweet, the happy married life, and the fruit rejoicing in the heart, we tried to outline these elegant scenes in the memory. Rustic wood, warm cotton, tea table with modern metal texture, in the fusion of tradition and modernness, we wanted to find the balance and the warm memories of cultural origin.

A quiet room full of tea flavor belonging to the corner is the precious enjoyment. None luxury is better than a mansion to reflect the reputation, strength and taste of a person or a family. In the class, health, comfort, taste, courtesy and other five levels reshape the essence of "elegant and luxurious life". Every spatial detail carries the culture, art, taste, the attitude of life and the pursuit of beauty.

因为美，我们便可以继续前行。

——蒋勋

在这个417平方米的空间里，我们试图对话古今，寻找一种平衡的美，于这一室中呈现我们对美的理解与追求。庄子有言"天地有大美而不言"，认为一切自然，不为利害得失所累，既合规律又合目的的统一，即为大美。然而所有的美，所有的艺术最终都体现为人，所以当你触摸一片叶，饮一席茶，听风从林中穿过，便可以感受到美，便可以寻着前行的意义。

忽一夜冬雪，万千雪白，清晨的第一份惊喜，王孙公子们亭台赏雪、湖面踏冰、孩童们雪中嬉戏，丫鬟们忙碌着清理廊道积雪……好不美丽的场景，仿佛听到欢声笑语传来，那一年繁荣的圆明园正在上演怎样美丽的故事？

中式屏风的雅致，配合欧式线条的硬朗，极富质感的餐椅和丝质地毯，让整个餐厅仪式感中不乏轻松和舒适。听风、吟茶、圆月腊梅、琴瑟和鸣，欣喜于心的果实，我们试图勾勒出记忆里风雅的画面，质朴的木、温暖的棉麻、带有现代气息金属质感的茶几，在传统与现代的融汇中，我们想找出平衡和文化根源的亲切记忆。

"素瓷传静夜，芳气满闲轩"，一室宁静，满室茶香，归属于一隅，更是现实难得的享受。没有什么奢侈品比豪宅更能体现一个人或一个家族的声望、实力与品位了，在圈层、健康、舒适、品味、礼遇等五大层面重塑"雅奢生活"的精髓，每一个空间细节，都承载着文化、艺术、品味、生活的态度和对美的追求。

Beauty has no connection with right and life. When we set aside prejudices, we will find, discover and create what we insist and what we keep doing with passionate emotions, and also we will break off the ruler measuring others all the time with an open and humble heart. Then the real "beauty" will appear in the eyes.

　　美与权利无关，美与生死无关。抛开成见与偏见，怀着炽热的情感去寻找、去发现、去创造我们所坚持的和一直在做的事，怀着坦诚与谦卑的心，折断时刻都在衡量他人的尺子，真正的"美"便会呈现在眼前。

禅境文心 诗意栖居

LIVING IN A VILLA FULL OF ZEN FLAVOR WITH A LITERARY HEART

项目名称 | 西安·荣禾清凉山居叠墅

设计公司 | SCD（香港）郑树芬设计事务所

主案设计师 | 郑树芬、徐圣凯

软装设计师 | 杜恒、丁静

项目地点 | 陕西西安

项目面积 | 407 ㎡

主要材料 | 进口墙纸、大理石、手工编织藤、
定制铁艺通花、木地板等

摄影师 | 张骑麟

设计理念 | DESIGN CONCEPT

Zen believes that "nothing is what is existing there." The "less" in the material seeks the "more" in the spirit, that is, people are awe of nature, but it is also a subtle manifestation of the spiritual temperament.

The wood carving in the foyer is the signboard in the old time. The carving is not elaborate but interesting, like carving a story of a master having a study tour with his disciple. The painting on the wall was originally from a Korean artist with the sun, clouds, water, rocks, mountains, pines, bamboos and fungus on it. In Asian cultures, the turtles, cranes and deer are considered the symbols of longevity. The painting with the strong color tone and exquisite technique, combines with the rough and rustic handmade clay pots. We try to integrate a multi-element culture of Asian to shape a residential space with emotional temperature.

Qing Liang Mountain is located in a park of Xi'an city. The landscape of stacked villas is elegant and pleasant, and one can fell the rhythm of nature between breath and spit. "Back to nature and life itself, we will find the beauty everywhere, and it is the starting point of life aesthetics." We will start from the "starting point", introducing the natural beauty into life and finding the essence of life. At the same time, we will integrate the Zen aesthetics into it, feeling the philosophy and aesthetic taste of life in a natural, poetic, quiet and tranquil place.

In Southeast Asian culture, the emotion of Buddha is not only faith, but also the hope and power of that smile whether it is in the peaceful world or the wartime. In the *The Beauty of Angkor,* Jiang Xun had mentioned what the meaning of Buddha to the people in the war is that a touch of serene smile gives them the courage to live. "All the expressions have become the past as if a lotus rising from a pool of sludge. That smile becomes the only expression on the heights above the city, containing love and hate, transcending life and death. Through a long time, the smile was passed to future generations."

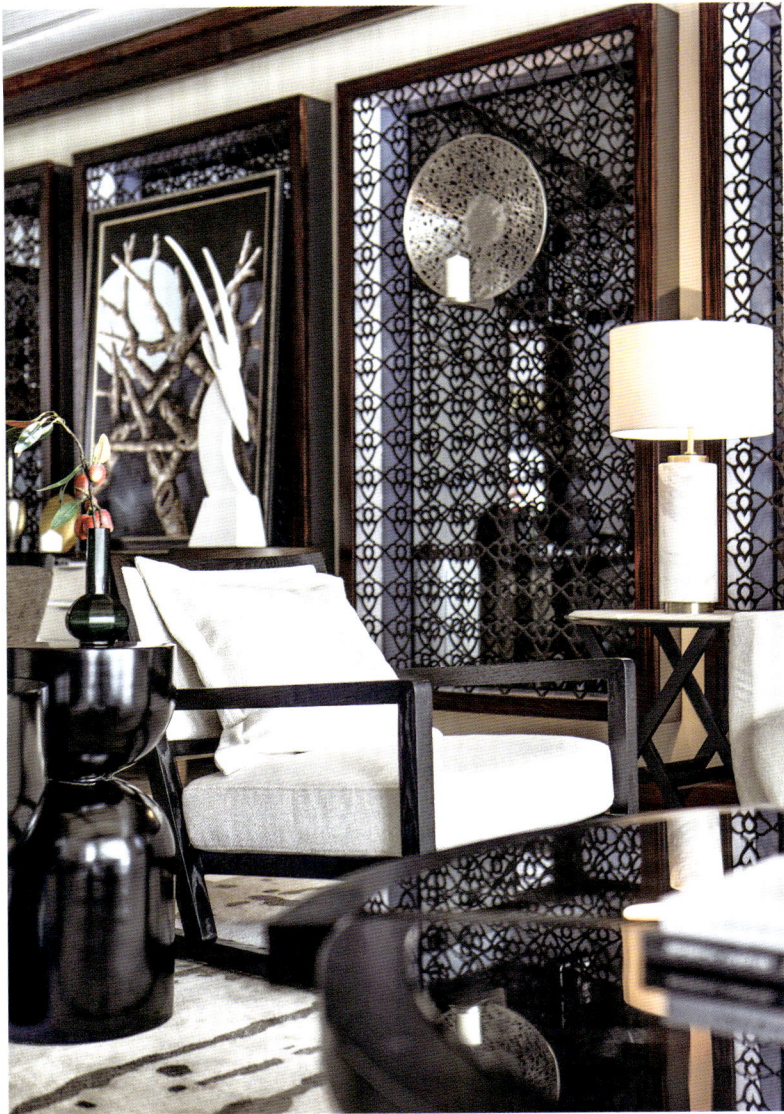

"山间残雪草争春，归来说与待花人"。禅认为"无即是有"，用物质上的"少"，去寻求精神上的"多"，即是人对自然的敬畏，也是一种含蓄的精神气质体现。

玄关处的木雕是淘来的旧时门头，雕刻不算精细，亦有一番趣味，像是刻画的一个师父与弟子游学中的故事。玄关墙壁的画，原出自一位朝鲜艺术家，太阳、云、水、岩石、山脉、松树、竹子、真菌、龟、鹤和鹿，在亚洲文化里被认为都是长寿的象征，色调浓厚，笔触精致，与粗糙质朴的手工陶罐相组合，我们尝试用亚洲多元素文化融合，塑造带有情感温度的居住空间。

清凉山居位于西安市区一个公园内，叠墅园林景观清雅宜人，一呼一吸，一吐一纳间亦可感受到自然的韵律，"回到大自然，回到生活本身，发现无所不在的美，就是生活美学的起点"，我们将从"起点"开始，将自然大美引入生活，寻找生活的本质，同时将禅意美学汇入其中，在自然诗意，清净恬淡中感受到人生的哲学与审美趣味。

在东南亚文化中对佛的情感不仅仅是信仰，无论是现世安稳或是战乱流年，那一抹微笑就是希望与力量。蒋勋在《吴哥之美》所写到的战乱中的人们，佛与他们的意义，就是那一抹安详的微笑给予他们活着的勇气。"一切的表情——成为过去，仿佛从污泥的池沼中升起一朵莲花，那微笑成为城市高处唯一的表情，包容爱恨，超越生死，通过漫长岁月，把微笑传递给后世"。

The living room and the dining room are connected by the design of the sloping roof, paved with plain wallpaper, rendering a relaxed and comfortable sense like in a holiday. The furnishing of dining room continues a reclusive natural aesthetics. The stump moving back from the forest with a little carving, allocating with a transparent glass becomes a dining table. The rough linen, the random branches in the vase, matching with the exquisite tableware and sculpture, this is the unrestricted vacation and natural aesthetic form in our heart.

Tea culture originated from China, while the Zen tea was epitomized by the Japanese tea ceremony. Chanting meditation is a practice, and tea ceremony is also a practice. The tea ceremony is a collection of Zen, architecture, interior, ikebana, cooking and other subjects. I had read the biography of Sen no Rikyuu, the tea master in Japan whose lifelong pursuit of tea ceremony and beauty has been a kind of obsession. Eventually, he died of the sword of power and jealousy, but never

regretted his pursuit of beauty. This elegant room full of tea fragrance is our pursuit of Zen tea and hope of natural and interesting life.

This unique entrance cabinet makes people a little excited, using an exquisite technique to express the briskness and the leisurely state of King vividly. We can feel its power yet not losing the attitude of vacation.

The design of whole master bedroom is elegant and hazy, without jumping colors but only the comfortable gray and reclusive green. The landscape painting behind the bed is delicate and ethereal, seemingly tangible but invisible, creating a comfortable and leisure space of Zen aesthetics. "It is boring where has a moon without clouds". Comparing with the full moon in a cloudless sky, the secluded moon shaded by the clouds is more adorable. This is not only a flavor of Zen but also a favor of implicit beauty in Asian culture.

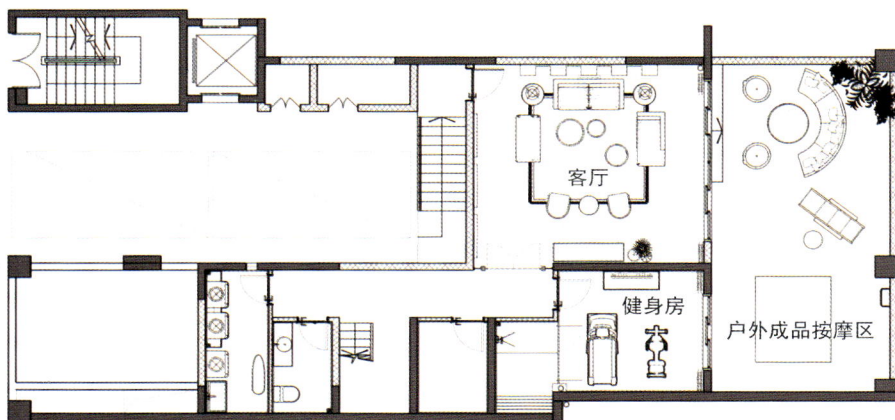

客餐厅相连的坡屋顶设计，铺以质朴的编制墙纸，给人置身度假的轻松舒适感。餐厅的陈设延续了隐逸的自然美学，树林里搬回来的树墩，稍加雕琢，配上一块通透的玻璃便是一张桌，粗犷的麻，花瓶里随意的树枝，配以精巧的餐具及雕塑，这便是我们心中不受约束的度假和自然美学形式。

茶文化发源于中国，而将禅茶集大成者的确是日本的茶道，念经坐禅是修行，茶道亦然。茶道集禅、建筑、室内、花道、烹饪等各种学科为一体。之前读日本茶道宗师"千利修"的传记，毕生对茶道和对美的追求已然是一种执念，最终死于权势与嫉妒的剑，却终不悔对美的追求。这一室的清雅与茶香，便是我们对禅茶的追求和对自然妙趣生活的期寄。

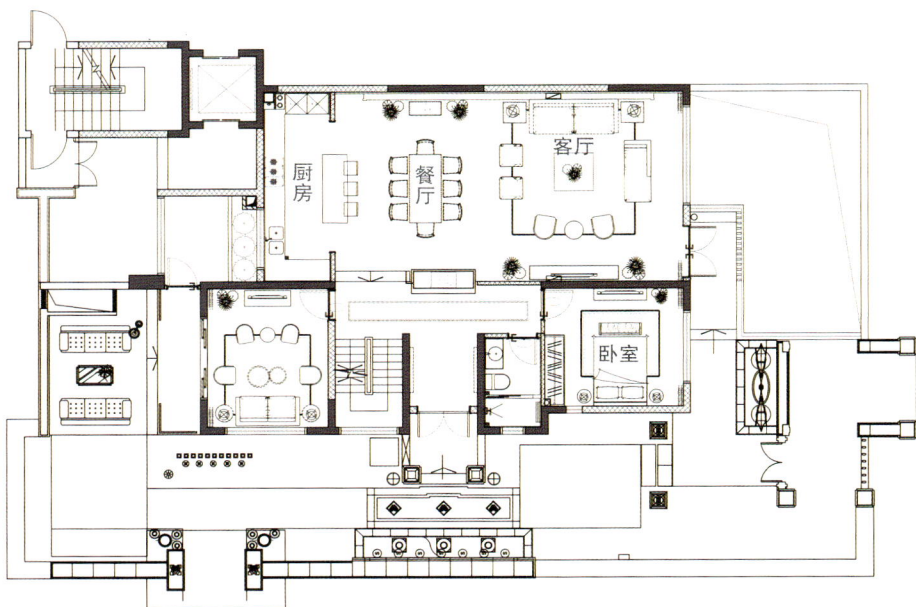

这个别具一格的玄关柜让人有点小兴奋，精致笔触，将王者的灵气和悠闲慵懒的状态表达的淋漓尽致，我们既可以感知力量，也没失去度假的态度。

整个主卧的设计清雅而朦胧，没有跳跃的色彩，只有舒适的灰、隐逸的青，床背后的山水画既精致又缥缈，似有形却无形，营造出一个休闲舒适的禅意美学空间。"有月无云枯无味"，比起万里无云天空下的满月，层云掩映下的幽静之月更惹人怜爱。这亦是一份禅意，也是亚洲文化对含蓄美的青睐。

The incomplete and lonely feeling of urban can be found here. The plain white and the flying red-crowned crane remind me of the verse that is "A stork's shadow flit across the chilly pool" in *A Dream in Red Mansions*. Can such an elegant scene evoke a moment of poetry and emotion?

In the small basement, the pure white linen, ink-liked table and round rattan, every material is carefully organized, and the comfort becomes the only language in this space.

"In people's haunt I build my cot; of wheel's and hoof's noise I hear not. How can it leave me no trace? Secluded heart makes a secluded place". If you are in a paradise with a confused mind, you also cannot be contented. Only the inner peace can make one feel the beauty of life. Beauty is not restricted by any form or symbol that is not only a flavor of Zen but also an attitude of life. We can not escape from the urban, but we can create a paradise in the deep of our heart carefully.

都市残缺清寂的感觉，在这里找到了，素净的白，振翅的仙鹤，让我想起《红楼梦》"寒塘渡鹤影"的诗句来，这样优雅的场景或许能勾起住客片刻的诗意和情感吧？

不算大的地下室，纯净的白麻，水墨般的案几，藤的圆润，每一个物料，都是用心组织的画面，舒适成为空间唯一的语言。

"结庐在人境，而无车马喧，问君何能尔，心远地自偏。"若身在世外桃源，心却杂乱，亦不能自得，内心的平静才能感悟到生活的大美。美，不拘于任何形式或符号，这便是一种禅意，更是一种生活的态度，我们逃离不了都市，却可以用心塑造属于我们心灵深处的世外桃源。

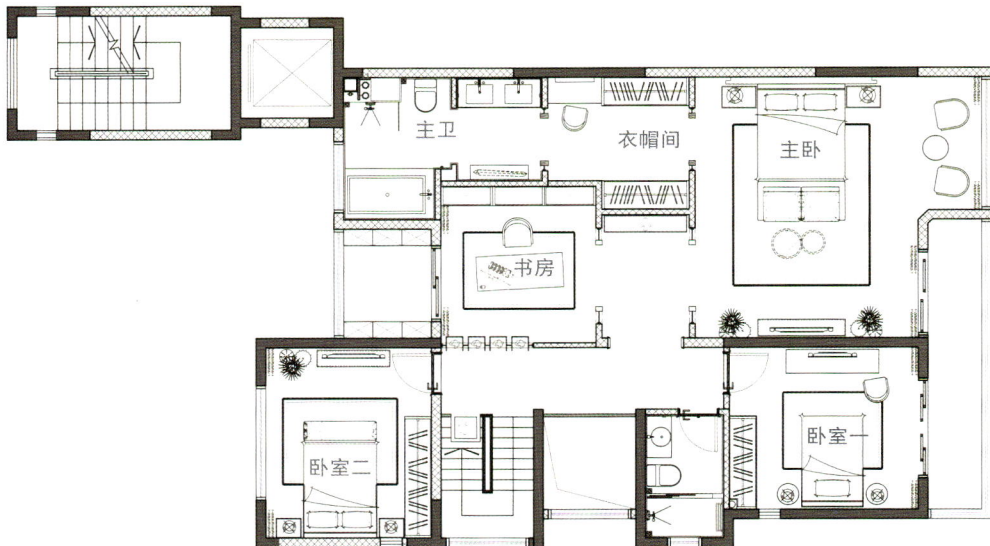

再现电影场景，享受设计之美

REAPPEARING THE MOVIE SCENE,
ENJOYING THE BEAUTY
OF DESIGN

视界对话葛晓彪

金元门设计
创始人兼艺术总监

葛晓彪
Ge Xiaobiao

随性而至，营创生活品质

获得荣誉

2016年 年度国际影响力设计师奖

2016年 入选Best中国100设计

2016年 金堂奖年度最佳设计

2016年 法国双面神大奖室内设计类最高奖金奖

2015年 加拿大蒙特利尔GRANDSPRIX DU DESIGN大奖金奖提名

2015年 法国双面神大奖室内设计类最高奖金奖

2015年 APDC亚太室内设计精英邀请赛杰出设计奖

2015年 第二届澳门国际"金莲花"杯设计大师邀请赛方案类银奖

2015年 入选Best 50中国最佳设计

2015年 第三届金创意年度十大最具影响力设计师奖

2014年 第十届中国国际室内设计双年展优秀奖

葛老师您好！我们知道，您是2011年从广告平面设计跨界到室内设计的，这当中有什么原因吗？您当时对室内设计有没有比较清晰的认识？

葛晓彪： 那一年，一个偶然原因，我尝试做了几个室内设计项目，被发表在当地的媒体上，自此以后作品开始得到越来越多业内人士的瞩目和好评，就这样开始了我的设计之路。当时我对室内设计没有清晰的概念和想法，只是把自己的心中所想通过室内这个媒介表达出来，觉得尝试每一种不同的创意并能最后落地很有意思，至于什么章法或是风格取向，完全没这样的概念，就这样一路走了过来。

您的作品带有浓厚的文化艺术气息，这跟您的平面设计经历有关吗？平面与室内设计有什么样的相互作用？

葛晓彪： 在做室内设计之前，我从事了十几年的平面广告设计工作，平面设计较之室内设计最大的感触是我们设计的每一则广告都需要标新立异，需要夺人眼球的与众不同，所以在创意上或是色彩上都会有很激情的碰撞；而转换到做室内设计时，我沿袭了平面广告一贯的做法，将涉及的新鲜元素更多地注入到案例中。我要求每一处细节都迸发新的灵感，创作出具有自己特色的作品，才能不断超越自己。这些年我一直都以广告的要求去梳理自己，做不重复的作品案例，因为跨界的路真的需要付出比旁人更多的努力，才能收获成长中的喜悦。值得高兴的是，在我坚持原创道路的同时，也让客户认可了我的设计思路，并设计出了我心中所想的每一套都与众不同的理想家园，让他们为之动容。

用色大胆、前卫、令人惊艳是您作品的特色，能和我们谈谈在选择和运用色彩上如何把握尺度吗？

葛晓彪： 我从广告设计转型而来，广告要求的就是闪亮、富有创意，而我用了广告的平面手法去对待立体空间，所以才会有这样彩色的画面；另外我本人又很喜欢看迪士尼动画大片，里面的场景让我沉醉，也是我创作的源泉，比如说动画片《冰雪奇缘》，以蓝调为背景，通过不同的色彩对比、变换，讲述和布局故事的情节，一幕幕都把握得非常到位。我希望我所表达的每一个空间都能有电影场景般的梦幻，让人心醉，这也是我一直以来追求的电影色，也就是我心心念念想要传达到位的色彩度。

"无设计不创意，无创意不设计"是您对设计的感悟，怎样才能做到每一套作品都充满创意和想象力？

葛晓彤：很多时候我在一进入到项目空间时，脑海里已经闪现出要呈现给人的画面，我希望是有那种电影场景的效果，而电影的画面感需要每一个场景都得到不断的完善和表现。我在落地项目的时候就把自己当做是一位导演，要完成生活中的每一个细节，就要考虑到如何把要表达的故事情节和每一个想象的空间变成现实的存在，自己也会琢磨如何将每一个创意变成一个又一个的可能。

您的作品能带给观者极大的视觉享受，同时又能极好地满足居者的生活体验需求，在这个过程中，您怎么兼顾视觉触感以及实用性、舒适度？

葛晓彤：我认为做设计不仅仅要美观，同时还要兼顾实用和舒适，这是做设计本该遵循的原则。设计源于生活又高于生活，所以我也是不断地在生活中进行提炼，从身体力行的方方面面去感知，从而带出最符合当下的生活方式。这是从一个设计师的角度，又是一个主人的角度，把该捕捉到的细节问题全方位地去解决并完善。

您凭借英伦摩登风格作品在国内外获得多项大奖，后现代风格作品在国内设计圈刷屏，国内外不乏挖掘、模仿、学习您作品之人，您是怎么理解这种现象的？

葛晓彤：其实我个人还是能理解这样的方式的，在还没形成特定思路和想法的时候，需要借鉴外力，让自己的案例做得圆满一点。但随着时间的推移和自身的成长，就需要更加关心案例背后的东西，模仿和学习最好作为一个参考，更多的是加入自己的元素和理念，这样一脉相承的案例才更有说服力和可塑性，也能在无形中形成自己的语言，传播给每一位爱美人士。

能跟我们聊聊目前国内室内设计行业所处的阶段吗？

葛晓彤：我认为室内设计已经经历了一个阶段，未来需要设计师更好地用时间和经验去沉淀一些东西，不要为了设计而设计。随着国际化进程的加快，很多的境外设计师被引进来，若是我们没有一个清晰的脉络顺序和匠人精神，很难做出有新意的作品，也就很难在高速发展的时代中脱颖而出，这也是我所担心的一件事。我希望有更多的人走出去，走向国际舞台；也希望有更多的人去提升自己，这样我们才能把中国的原创设计做得更有生命力。

您经常会参加一些讲座与交流会，喜欢并善于分享，对于正从事设计的年轻人，您有没有一些经验可以参考？

葛晓彤：我因为偶然跨入这个设计圈，一路走来有很多的心得与体会，但并非有可以速成的技巧或方法，只能说做设计需要的是一种感知力、动手力以及思考力。我们学习知识也是如此，到底讲求先难后易还是先易后难，我觉得对于正在学习的设计师们，可以让自己的思维更加活跃一点，更加具有创意一点，不用怕做错。很多时候就需要一些天马行空的想象并付诸行动，才能让原本认为不可能的事变成可能，所以说设计需要大胆尝试，需要从微小的细节处感知生活的每一种不同的可能。

"初心"是一个倾注着内心细腻情感的词语，是一个强调情怀的词语，也是一个很个性化的词语，您常说"不忘初心"中的"初心"具体指什么呢？

葛晓彤：我认为的初心就是童真，就如同毕加索所说，"我在十几岁时画画就像个大师，但我花了一辈子学习怎样像孩子那样画画"，因为那份率真和质朴才是整个作品的精髓所在。所以我时常这么想，若是哪一天做出了感动我自己内心的案例，我就不再做设计了。

每个人都有一份家乡情怀，对于您的家乡宁海在室内设计上的发展您有关注吗？

葛晓彤：我的家乡宁海其实在室内设计这一块还是比较落后的，但我始终希望我的案例能带动家乡的设计，让这份美可以传播给更多的人，让他们享受到美带来的无穷乐趣。

通过您的微博动态，我们能了解到您和您的团队是一个非常有意思的组合。在您心里，您的团队是什么样的？怎么样能让团队更好地成长？

葛晓彤：我的团队也还在慢慢地成长阶段，需要不断提升和历练。在我的团队眼里，可能我是一个比较精益求精的老师，不断去挖掘各种可能，否定每一个即将成行的思路，让他们用发散性的思维去创想各种新思路。当然前期可能会很痛苦，但在最后效果呈现时，他们也会为这样的执着而感受到我的良苦用心。

A MODERN AND ARTISTIC HOME

摩登艺术·家

设计公司丨金元门设计公司

设 计 师丨葛晓彪

项目地点丨宁波

项目面积丨1000 ㎡

摄 影 师丨刘鹰

设计理念 | DESIGN CONCEPT

Space is fulfilled with an elegant temperament, demonstrates the imaginative imagination and creativity of the designer everywhere, tells the story, and transfers ideas, like the affection along with the heart. It is lasting.

The entrance fulfills with the sense of lines, and makes people curious instantly. The decorative plastic materials in the living room are served for the overall panel, blending the classic and modern elements perfectly. The off-white human body painting echoes with the large-scale male sculpture. The side seam of the mirror with gold foil fuses with the bead-shaped golden chandelier in one. The round bulb allocating with brass material forms a striking contrast with the top of the French raised pattern, which is fashionable and wonderful. The modern shark fin sectional sofa coupled with seemingly random fishing lights decoration make space more vitality and modern.

The metallic chandelier in dining room echoes with gold branches. One can feel the charm of dining area sitting on the oval dining table.

The radian of stairs pillars is elegant; it can lead people's vision back to origin through the oil painting fused with fabrics and oil painting elements, like a woman dressed in costumes walking down. It is charming. The cyan female sculpture makes the space full of fun, and the luster of golden shell material seats are special, complementing the abstract female's paintings on the white panel. It is like being in a palace of Art.

Bookshelves, light perception, sculpture materials, and snowflake-shaped top surface, every visual angle of these sceneries is picturesque and captures the eye which is quiet yet not lonely. The tweedle is melodious, and the black paint piano beating notes make the space vacant and full of artistic conception. Black matte panel with a little wood pattern mixed with the golden copper strip is calm and classy. The yellow-green color lumps of abstract painting brighten the dark color tone space, and the shell-shaped marble wall lamp restraints the cool and magnificent space perfectly.

Similarly, the lounge is connected with the color lumps. The designer used orange velvet sofa collocating with claret-colored rotating seat, dusty pink seats and light green carpet, which make the blue space fresh. The folding window not only can be used as decoration, but also can block some lights which are win-win, and can have a leisurely life and mood.

The design of bedroom is inspired by the British gentlemen and the wind and sunshine of Mediterranean. In the former, the designer used arc background modeling to foil space temperament, and the simple lines allocating with leather hard decoration as embellishment which is simple and neat. Gray fishbone shaped collage floor with traces of years polished exudes a uniquely broad and inclusive charm. In the latter, the designer used blue and white color as expansion, and the bed curtain in palace style at the bedside allocating with the gauze curtain and feather decoration in the same color, which is light, graceful and romantic. The changing room and bathroom are also colorful. Different colors and shapes create an elegant, unique and stunning feeling of the whole space ingeniously.

　　空间里弥漫着高雅的气质，处处表现设计师天马行空的想象和创意，诉说故事与传递思想，如曲水流觞后的情随心动，耐人寻味。

　　进门处充满线条感，瞬间令人心生好奇。客厅的装饰塑材为整体的护墙服务，古典与现代元素完美融合。灰白的人体挂画与大型的男性雕塑相呼应，金箔的镜子边缝与珠状的金色吊灯宛若共生，圆灯泡搭配黄铜材质，与顶面的法式浮雕花纹形成鲜明对比，时尚、妙不可言。现代感极强的鲨鱼鳍组合沙发，加上看似随意的钓鱼灯摆设，空间更具活力与摩登气息。

餐区的金属质感吊灯与金枝相互映衬，坐于椭圆形的餐桌旁，便感受到餐区的韵味。楼梯的柱子弧度优雅，通过布艺和油画元素融合而来的油画让人的视觉回到原点，如有女子身着华服款步而下，光彩动人。青色的女子雕塑让空间充满趣味，金色贝壳材质的座椅光泽特别，与白色护墙板上的抽象女子画作相得益彰，令人犹如置身艺术殿堂。

书柜、光感、雕塑材质、雪花造型顶面，各视觉角度的景致皆如画，夺人眼球，静而不寂。琴声悠扬婉转，黑色烤漆钢琴跳动的音符令空间空灵，富有意境。黑色亚光护墙透出些许木纹，夹杂金色铜条，沉稳、有档次。黄绿色块的抽象画点亮暗色调的空间，贝壳状的大理石壁灯又恰到好处地克制了空间的冷艳。

休闲室同样通过色块进行衔接，设计师用橘黄的天鹅绒沙发搭配紫红色的旋转座椅、藕粉色座椅、淡绿的地毯，让蓝色的空间变得鲜活。折叠窗既可作为装饰，亦可挡一部分光线，一举两得，也滋生平和、闲适心境。

卧室的设计灵感分别源自英伦的绅士与地中海的和风煦日。在前者中，设计师用弧形背景造型来烘托空间气质，以简约的线条搭配皮质的硬包为点缀，简约利落。灰色鱼骨状拼贴地板带有岁月打磨的痕迹，散发着独特的博大与包容魅力。在后者中，设计师以蓝、白色调展开，在床头处采用宫殿式幔头，配上同色调纱幔、羽毛装饰物，轻盈、曼妙、浪漫非凡。更衣室与卫浴空间亦色彩纷呈，不一样的色素与造型巧妙地打造出整套空间的优雅别致和惊艳之感。

THE EXTREME HIGH-END GRAY

化繁为简 极致高级灰

项目名称 | 郁金花园
设计公司 | 金元门设计公司
设 计 师 | 葛晓彪
项目地点 | 浙江宁海
项目面积 | 240 ㎡

设计理念 | DESIGN CONCEPT

Entering the house, a neat gray space comes into sight, which is soft, calm, quiet and elegant. Considering the female owners, the designer harmonized partly purple color on the basis of the gray system, showing a more delicate and soft texture and sense.

The original staircase is located in the center of space, resulting in the effects of the area of living room and dining room and space line. So the designer adjusted the stairs to the northwest corner that it is located on a cross-shaped center line on the first floor, releasing the living room, dining room and leisure space. Combined with the double balcony and the layout of the air outlet and return air inlet of air condition, the ventilation and lighting of the room are greatly improved, and the vision in any position is excellent. At the same time, the designer expanded the function of the dining room with a table accommodating 12 people to meet the needs of owners dining with relatives, communication or having an afternoon tea, which can develop the communicative function of the dining area fully. While only a modernist geometric painting is used as the element of brightening space, the careful design of air outlet makes the decorative elements integrate with interior style well and enhances the comfort of space. Besides, all bedrooms are adjusted to the south side so that each space can enjoy the best view of the housing estate.

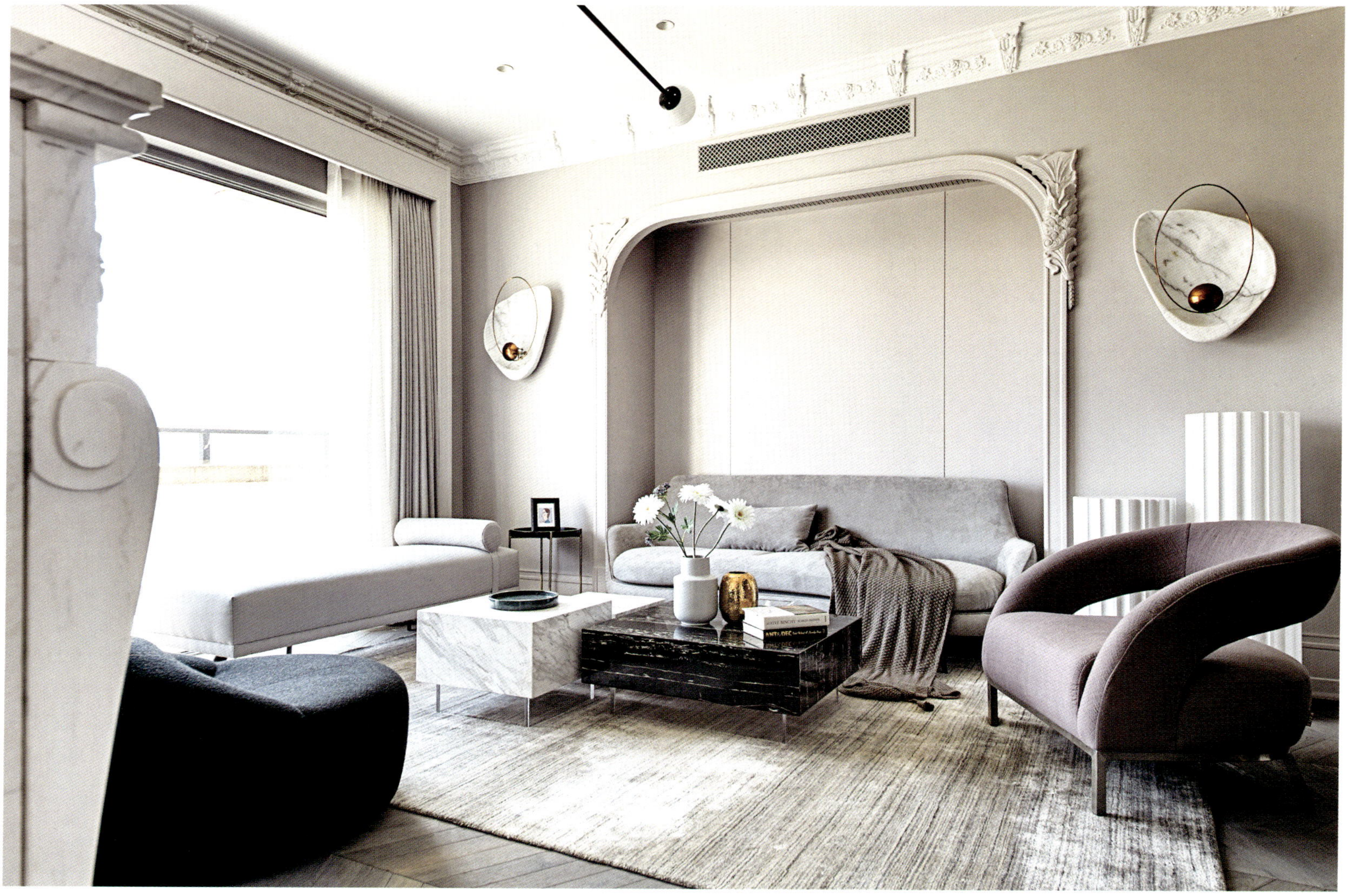

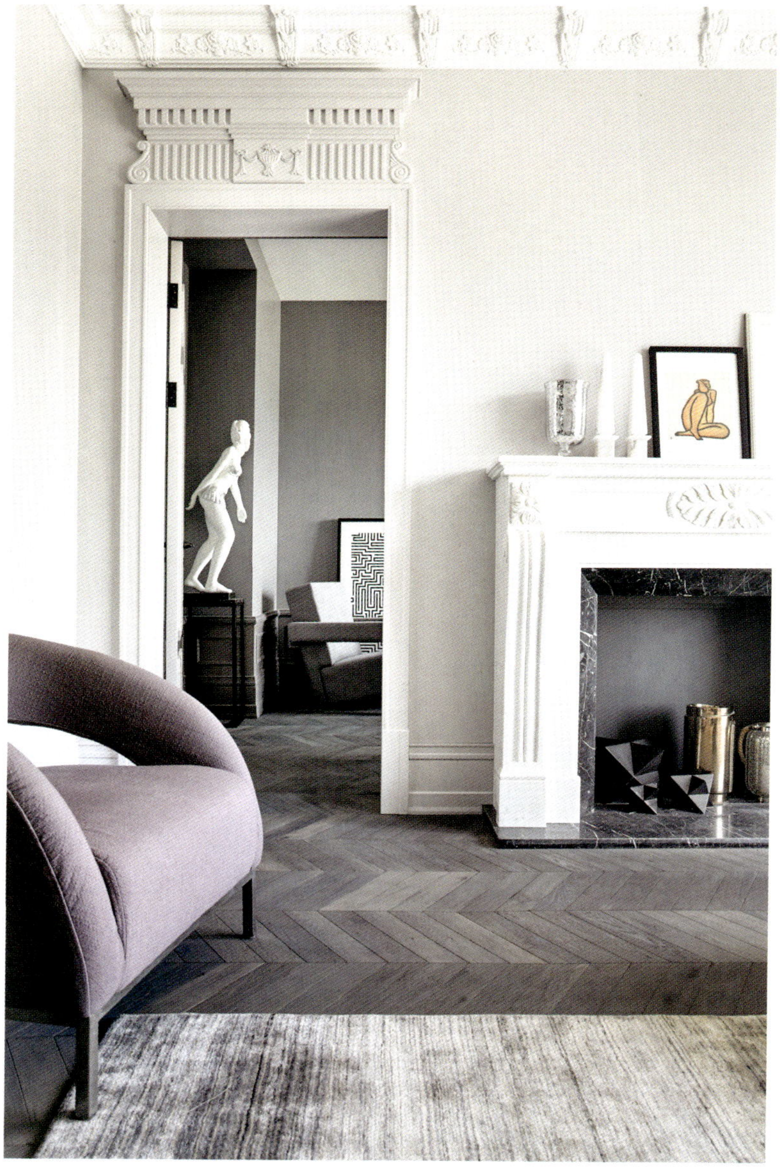

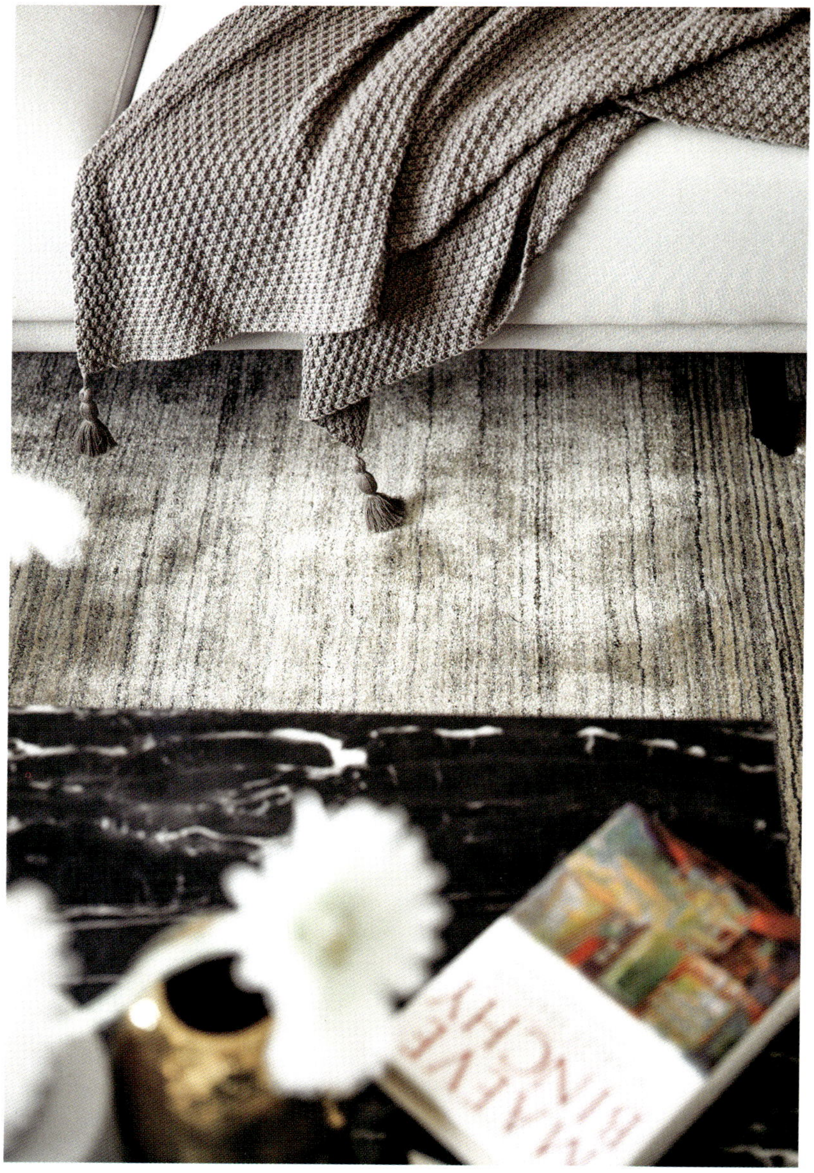
MAEVE BINCHY

厨房

设备阳台

餐厅

书房

客厅

露台

露台

客卫

储藏室

卫生间

老人房

衣帽间

主卧

卫生间

女儿房

卫生间

茶室

露台

The living room is in parallel with the dining room. Through the porch transition, the folding door is designed on both sides, which has a better coordination and can adjust the light quantities and air velocity appropriately. Dome lights are divided into two imbalanced placed light group both sides, which can make the whole living room balance. While the pole and beads in the middle of the space and tea table are interest and charm. The fireplace forms a good interaction with dome lamp and tea table, adding the aesthetic elements and increasing the fun of life. The sofa is creatively embedded in the background wall, leaving storage space for the next bedroom. At the same time, it creates a good spatial scale to make it have a better space experience.

Next to the living room, the study integrates with the activity room as a whole. The folding desk can enhance the degree of freedom of space, while the folding shutter window does not only adjust the light quantities but also does not affect ventilation. The designer placed the interesting ornaments on a carpet which can let the children sit on the ground to play, fully closing to the children's nature and innocence.

On the first floor, the bedroom is specially prepared for parents, so the overall color is deeper. The selection of wallpaper is environmental wallpaper, and the feather wall lamps on both sides of the bedside are gentle and warm, all of these can express their care and love for the elder. The public bathroom and the restroom of the bedroom are distributed under the stairs, reducing the arrangement of the whole space pipeline.

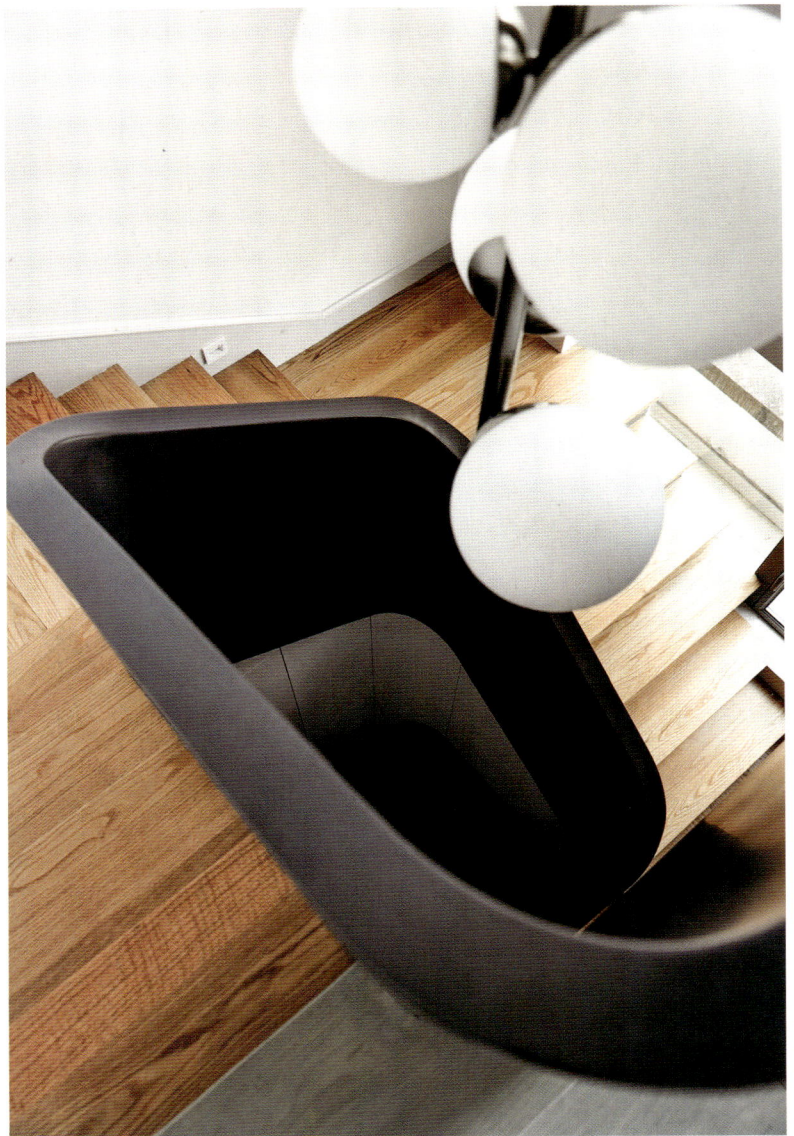

推门而入，眼前是一个干净利落的灰调空间，柔和、沉稳、宁静、雅致。为女业主考虑，设计师在灰色系的基础上调和部分紫色，呈现更为细腻和柔软的肌理与感观。

原先楼梯位于空间正中，导致客、餐厅的面积和空间动线受到影响，因而设计师将楼梯调整到西北角，使其位于一层十字布局的中心线上，释放客、餐厅以及休闲空间。结合双阳台、中央空调出风口与回风口的布局，空间的通风、采光得到极大改善，且任意位置的视野都十分出色。同时，设计师扩大餐区的功能，用12座的餐桌满足业主和亲友聚餐、交流或下午茶的需要，充分发挥餐区的交际功能。仅以一幅当代主义的几何画作为提亮空间的元素，对出风口做细节化处理，让装饰元素与室内风格融合统一，提升空间的舒适性。此外，所有卧室都被调整到南边，各空间都能欣赏小区的最好景观。

客厅与餐区位置平行，通过门廊过渡，两边设计折叠门，协调性较好，可适当调整进光量和空气的流速。顶灯为两头不均分的灯组，利用不均衡造就客厅整体的均衡，而灯杆和灯珠处于空间和茶几的中间点上，意趣巧妙。壁炉与顶灯、茶几形成良好的互动，增添审美元素，增加生活乐趣。沙发创意性地嵌在背景墙内，给隔壁卧室留出收纳空间，同时打造空间良好的尺度，使其具备更好的空间体验。

客厅隔壁的书房和活动室合为一体，可折叠的书桌提升空间的自由度，而折叠百叶木窗既调整进光量，又不影响通风。设计师将趣味摆件放在了一张地毯上，让来此的孩子可以坐在地上玩耍，充分贴近孩子的童真天性。

一楼的卧室为父母特意准备，所以整体色彩更深一些，壁纸选用环保壁纸，床头两侧的羽毛壁灯轻柔而温馨，处处表达对老人的关爱。公卫和卧室的卫生间镜像分布于楼梯下，减少整个空间的管线排布。

Up to the arc staircase, the design of creativity infiltrates silently in the details. The light from the North window leaves the shadow of people on the blank wall forming a dynamic decoration. The end of the porch is the sunshine room with a shelter gable which has a square gap on it. Slowly walking through it, one can have an excellent view of a natural variety of scenery picture scroll.

On the basis of different shades of the dominant color system, the designer gave rich details and humanistic connotations to the high-end gray color in the bedroom. The wallpaper of master bedroom with a Japanese Ukiyoe feeling represents exquisite details of contemporary aesthetics. The dressing table from Britain uses an arc for importing the tenderness and warmth of female into it. In the black and white color tone, the master bathroom with a layer of soft floating renders a dreamy atmosphere.

The quiet space with high-end gray needs to enrich the picture through furniture and furnishing. So on the selection of furniture, the designer used the gray color fusing with a background mainly, while the local vessels and flowers used the high saturation bright color as embellishments which can become a focal point and inject elegance and vitality into space.

　　沿弧形楼梯而上，设计的创意在细节中无声浸润。北窗的光在留白的墙面上留下人影，形成动态装饰。门廊的尽头是阳光房，一道山墙遮风挡雨，墙上开了一个方口，缓步走过，一幅自然百变的风景画卷便尽收眼底。

　　在不同灰度的主调色系的基础上，设计师在卧室中为高级灰赋予丰富的细节和人文内涵。主卧壁纸带有日系浮世绘的感觉，却呈现当代审美的精致细节。选自英国的梳妆台，用一条弧线将女性的柔美和温情导入空间。在黑白灰基调的主卫中，一层柔光浮动，梦幻气氛恍若天成。

　　宁静的高级灰空间，需要用家具和陈设艺术来丰富画面，故而设计师在大体量家具的选择上，以与背景融合的灰色调为主，而局部的器皿、花艺则以高饱和的亮色作为点缀，起到画龙点睛的作用，为空间注入优雅与活力。

The gray color in sight is not gray, and the sky blue what people said is the blue sky behind the white clouds in front of the balcony of this house. Looking at the mountain, the owner can see a column of dancing windmills. Abandoning the hustle and bustle of city life, coming back home, and facing the blue sky and mountains, you can breathe a wisp of fragrance, taste a poetic life, and enjoy a comfortable, lazy and cheerful mood.

　　眼前的灰不是灰，人们说的天空蓝，是这个家阳台前白云背后的蓝天。居者望向山的眼，能看见一列风车在起舞。抛却凡尘的喧嚣，回到家中，便可对着蓝天远山，呼吸一缕芬芳，品味生活的诗意，享受一份安逸、慵懒、愉悦的心情。

翁伟锴

伟格思室内设计
董事、设计总监

Neville Yung

设计源于背后的思考

获得荣誉

2013年 第八届中国国际建筑装饰及设计艺术博览会

2013年 国际环艺创新设计大赛"酒店空间设计一等奖"

2013年 国际环艺创新设计大赛"商业空间设计一等奖"

2013年 中国十佳商业规划及空间设计师

以人为本，专注设计
FOCUSING ON PEOPLE-ORIENTED AND DESIGN

视界对话翁伟锴

翁老师您好！我们知道，您很少出席公众活动，公众对您的了解也相对比较少，那在您看来，自己是一位什么样的人？在平时，您是如何定位您的工作和生活的？

翁伟锴：相对来说我是一个不善于交际应酬的人，因此更愿意把时间专注在工作上，也可以说是一个"工作狂"。工作与生活的平衡是非常重要的，工作时全力以赴，休假时专注于家庭生活，家庭始终是我认为的最大的后盾及支持。

您曾说设计是一种辅助"工具"，您是如何运用这一"工具"，以及希望达到什么样的效果？

翁伟锴：室内设计除了是"艺术"，也是"实用美学"。做设计的出发点和归宿均是为人和人际活动服务，即通常所言的"以人为本"。运用设计这一"工具"，我们将创新设计理念和人文艺术内涵融入其中，满足使用者对空间功能的需求以及对美学意境和形式的精神追求。

您和贵公司做的项目类型很多，包括酒店、会所、餐厅、样板间等，在这些项目中，您觉得样板房的设计价值是什么呢？

翁伟锴：样板房属于展示性空间，引领人们对生活的追求，体验家居生活、时尚潮流，带领人们在不断进步的新时代中进行生活体验，领悟新时代的生活品质，启发、引导甚至在一定程度上改变人们在其活动空间中的生活方式和行为模式。

当下，人们不仅要求空间要有奢华感，也不断追求舒适度，您怎么理解和把握这二者的关系？

翁伟锴：奢华感和舒适度，因人而异，见仁见智。环境的不同或生活背景的差异给体验者带来的空间感受均不相同。比如，地理位置有优势的空间，得天独厚的自然环境自成一派奢华，便可采取轻硬装重软装的设计手法，奢华、舒适点缀其中，相互映衬，反之亦然。用理性和睿智驾驭奢华，而非被奢华所困。

在住宅类项目的设计过程中，您是如何把握各个空间的设计的呢？

翁伟锴：在设计的过程中，我一般每个空间都会非常注重，既要考虑到刚需功能和精神功能的要求，更要遵循美学的原理，使得平面布局、空间比例均经过严谨推敲。对于空间光环境和视觉环境的采光与照明、色调和色彩配置、材料质地和纹理，以及地理气候等因素的考虑，都细致、深刻地反映了设计美学中的空间形体美、功能技术美、装饰工艺美。

您在设计中是比较关注现代风格的，那对于其中越发进入人们视野的后现代风格，您有什么想法和思考？

翁伟锴：后现代风格的设计我是非常喜欢的，它是一种没有特定的框架、范围和定义的室内设计风格。后现代风格打破了传统的设计思维，可以是中西古今的重建与融合，也可以是不对称、夸张、错位、变形等多元的设计表现手法，运用新时代的材料、工艺来创造全新的设计理念，将古典的设计重新演绎。

面对当今的房地产和设计行业的情况转变，您对未来有什么规划？

翁伟锴：这是一个热门话题，很多人都问过我相似的问题，曾在清华大学授课时，部分学生也提出过类似问题。准确地说，我更愿意讲房地产企业正在"进化""革新"，房地产企业通过改革及资源整合后催生出新类型项目，其市场范围非常巨大，对从事房地产行业的设计公司的要求更加专业及高效。我们公司有着多元化的设计背景，设计的项目包括房地产、酒店、餐饮、别墅、商业等类型，未来我们将继续发展多元化设计理念。

从业多年，对于设计，您最深刻的心得和收获是什么？

翁伟锴：回望过去20多年的设计生涯，是一个从零开始到得到各方认可的过程。至今，我仍是坚信以人为本的态度，同时专业扎实的功底、各方面经验的累积都是非常重要的。室内设计不能只单纯考虑"好看""创新"，更多的是要深层考虑整体的融合性，满足设计需求的同时，要将不同的设计素材结合，达至最佳的平衡。

迷人法式 匠心演绎

THE BEST INTERPRETATION OF CHARMING FRENCH STYLE

项目名称 | 香港置地约克北郡别墅样板间

设计公司 | 伟格思室内设计（北京）有限公司

设 计 师 | 翁伟锴、汤之军

软装设计 | 上海1921软装设计

项目地点 | 重庆

项目面积 | 500 ㎡

设计理念 | DESIGN CONCEPT

This case is a new French style, which is noble and elegant, advocating nature, pursuing the exquisite beauty of details, conveying a noble temperament.

On the plane layout, designers aimed to show the perfect romantic life style feelings. The first floor is the activity space, the close interaction among the open kitchen, living room and dining room representing the attention of the family and concerning the communication between family members. The second floor is a static floor for children's room and the elder's room. The elders have their hobby activity space and enjoy the happiness of a family union here. The third floor is the owner's room with a spacious bedroom, an independent and luxurious four-piece suite, a bathroom, an independent cloakroom and a study with terrace, which can show a romantic and unique quality of life. While the basement is a mixed family layer, which is the most characteristic. The light introduces the light ingeniously. And the space, with interest as the introduction, not only can satisfy the family member's interests but also fills with the perfect image of the growing child's future, hoping the child similarly likes the French culture and pursues the free life.

In the design of modeling, designers promised that each space has the interpretation of French culture. The stone mosaic medallion on the ground, the white fancy wall angle, the gypsum line on the top surface and the pursuit of the natural elements, all of these are the embodiments of romantic French style. The local modeling adopts the design of decorative columns which are exquisite and delicate, showing the preferences of the owner for French Rococo art.

The whole color tone is light and harmonious. The owner loves the cultural collision of French Rococo art and Chinese art, so that the usage of a large area hand-painted flower and birds wallpaper among three floors is outstanding, and meanwhile, it integrates with other fancy wall angle modeling to create an overall luxurious, elegant and delicate flavour.

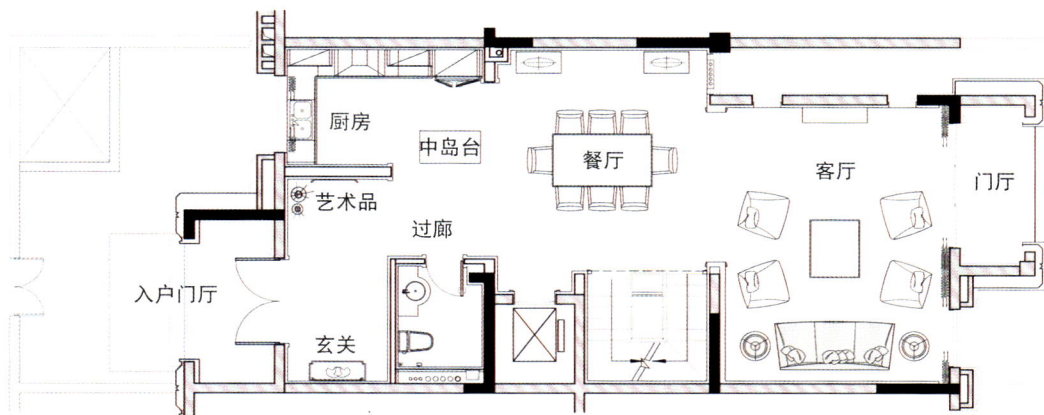

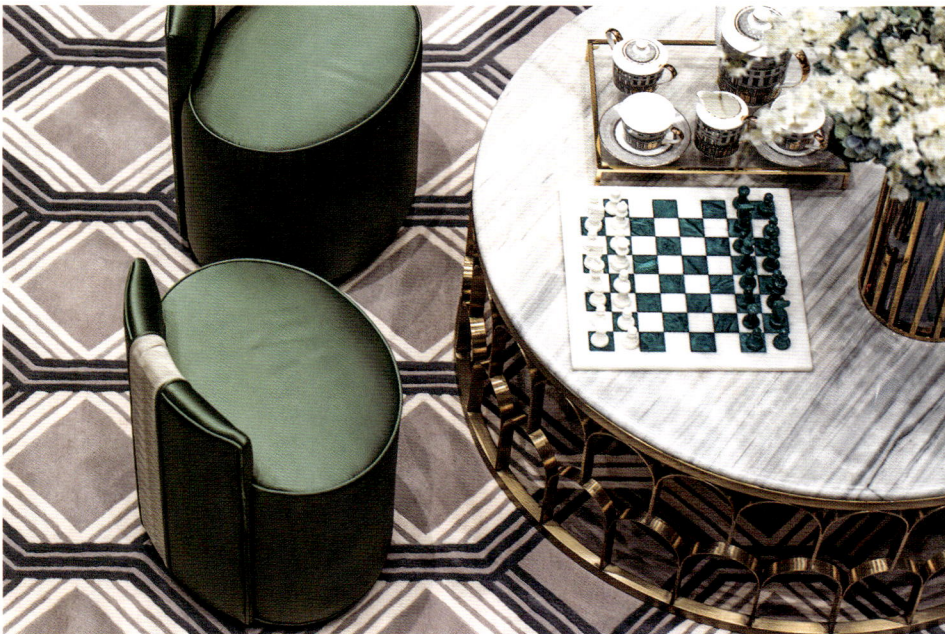

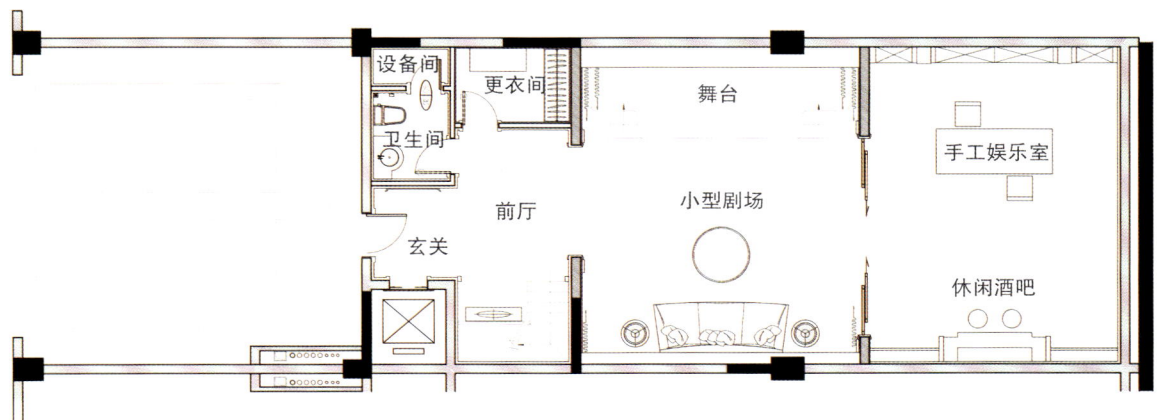

设备间

更衣间

舞台

卫生间

手工娱乐室

前厅

小型剧场

玄关

休闲酒吧

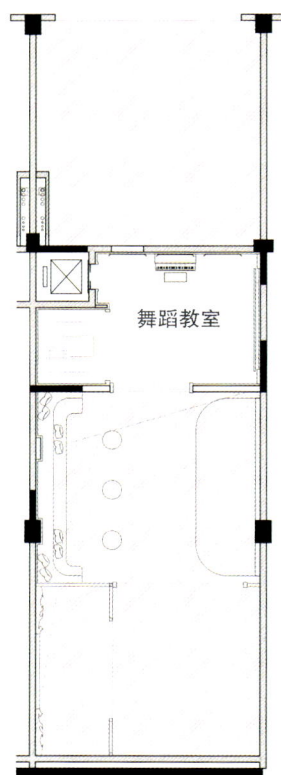

本案为新法式风格，高贵典雅，崇尚自然，追求细节精致之美，传达一种贵族气质。

平面布局上，设计师旨在表现完美浪漫的生活主义情怀。首层为活动空间，敞开式厨房、客厅与餐厅的近距离互动等体现对家庭的注重，关切家庭成员间的交流。二层为孩子房与老人房的静态层，老人在此有自己的爱好活动空间，且可享受天伦之乐。三层为业主自己的空间，敞亮的卧室，独立且奢华的四件套卫生间，独立的衣帽间，以及带有露台的书房，无处不体现浪漫独特的生活品位。而地下层是家庭混合层，最具特色，采光井巧妙引进光线，空间则以兴趣为引入，在满足家庭成员兴趣爱好的同时，更充满了对成长中的孩子未来的完美设想，希望他同样喜欢法兰西文化且追求自在生活。

造型设计上，设计师保证每个空间都有对法兰西文化的诠释。地面的石材拼花，墙面的白色花式线角，顶面的石膏花线，以及对自然元素的热烈追求，处处体现法式风格的浪漫情怀。局部造型运用了装饰角柱的设计，精致、细腻，展现出居者对产生于法国的洛可可艺术的喜好。

整体色调轻快、和谐。业主喜爱洛可可艺术与中国艺术的文化相撞，故而三层采用大面积手绘花鸟墙纸，特点突出，同时又与其他花式线角造型相融，营造整体奢华、典雅的精巧气息。

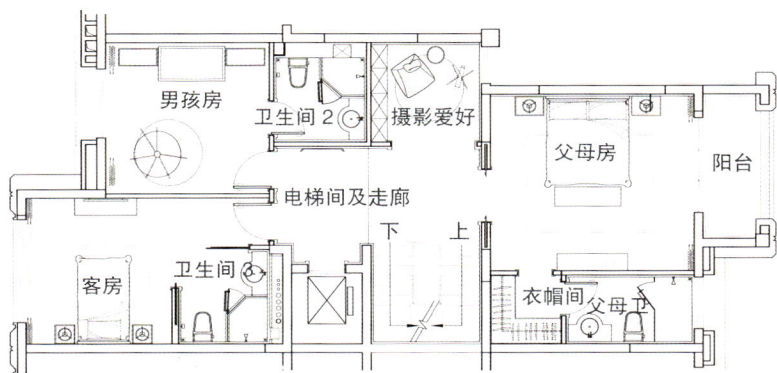

男孩房　　卫生间2　摄影爱好

　　　　　　父母房　　阳台

电梯间及走廊

　　　下　　上

客房　卫生间　　　　　　衣帽间　父母卫

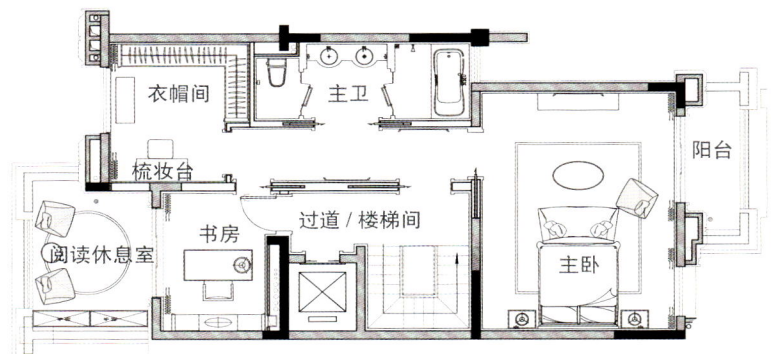

衣帽间　　　　主卫

梳妆台

阅读休息室　书房　过道/楼梯间　　阳台

　　　　　　　　　　　　　　　主卧

罗玉立

深圳市则灵文化艺术有限公司
创始人、设计总监

Luo Yuli
美是普遍的愉悦感受

获得荣誉

2016年 万科集团 优秀合作伙伴奖

2016年 星河第三空间 年度陈设艺术设计奖

2015年 金地集团 杰出贡献奖

2014年 金地集团 优秀合作伙伴奖

2013年 第三届亨特窗饰杯 中国软装100商业空间类优秀作品奖

2013年 金堂奖 年度优秀样板间/售楼处设计

美好生活的传递者
THE DELIVERER OF A GOOD LIFE

视界对话罗玉立

罗老师好，今年是您从事设计行业的第二十个年头，做设计这么多年，最让您感触、感动的地方是什么？

罗玉立：十几年前，我们组织同事去美国看高点展，那是个只有6万人口的小镇，但是我们住过的每一个房子都非常美，参展完我们搬到了远离市区的乡下去居住了一段时间，推开每一个房间的门，都能感受到主人对生活的享受，和他们对美好居住环境的审美品味。这些年中国的房地产业得到了极大的发展，但即使是千万级的豪宅，居住环境和生活品质还远没有达到西方国家的水平。

您当初决定成立"则灵艺术",也是出于这样的初衷吗?

罗玉立:正是因为看到这样的差距,所以我们希望用设计来服务于中国人的家居生活。从美国的家居产业来看,他们展现出来的是一个以居住者为中心的,可以拎包入住的全产业链形态,设计整合了家具、窗帘、地毯、日用品。但中国目前的形态,这些部分是剥离的,由完全不同的供应商和品牌提供,没有人来做整合。所以我们的目的就是利用我们的经验和专业能力来做一个整合者,为一流的房地产企业设计展示样板房,这可以影响到尽可能多的购房人群,为他们提供美好生活的样本。

您的设计作品就像您坚持的设计理念一样,让人有非常舒适愉悦的感受,尤其是在色彩的运用上,既出彩又和谐,常常产生惊艳的效果。您是怎么做到的呢?对于每个项目在色彩的选择上,您有什么搭配标准吗?

罗玉立:从技术层面来讲,大部分美术学院毕业的学生都能够做到良好的色彩搭配。但是如何运用这些理论来达到自己的目标,不同的人观点差别会很大。当我们确定了自己的目标是"设计传递生活的愉悦"的时候,我们就会以这个为准则,就是让人感觉得到生活的快乐,所以情感是很重要的指引因素。

作为女性设计师是不是对色彩的选择上会更细腻一些?表现在哪些方面?

罗玉立:大部分女性设计师在对美好生活的想象能力上会优于男性设计师。女性对生活的理解,和她们对美好生活的细腻感受,可以帮助她们所组合的这些色彩给人带来愉悦感。

如今在中国室内设计行业女性设计师稳占一定比例,您觉得设计过程中,女性设计师的优势在哪里?如何才能最大发挥女性设计师的优势?

罗玉立:我们公司目前女性设计师比例超过60%,她们都是我们用心遴选出来的杰出人才,有着一流的审美能力,同时又拥有极为细腻的情感和对美好生活的观察力,我们

培养她们注重体验和情景,鼓励她们把这些能力注入到设计作品里,创造唯美的、令人感动的生活场景。

您设计的项目比较偏爱法式风格,而且擅长,很多比较大的别墅项目您都是做的法式风格,是因为您本身是比较喜欢浪漫的人吗?关于法式风格的设计有没有一些心得可以跟我们分享一下呢?

罗玉立:我们经常去法国旅游和看展,每年都和公司同事一起去看巴黎展,我们都比较喜欢法式风格。从整个设计史的角度来看,法式风格也是最稳定的一种风格,富有优雅和浪漫的气息,同时又跟时尚潮流融合的非常紧密。我们设计的法式,并不是古典法式的沿袭,而是将它当代化,并与中国人的生活去融合,呈现了一部分人对这种生活方式的审美。

跟您合作的大部分都是比较大的上市房地产企业,则灵艺术也一直致力于样板房室内设计,如何做到样板房设计适应消费者需求?做样板房设计的关键是什么?

罗玉立:则灵选择只与国内最一流的上市房地产企业合作,是因为这些公司有着一流的人才和管理能力,他们理解未来社会发展的趋势,也认可我们团队对这一问题的理解和价值。则灵的设计,一直都以社会学和心理学研究为基础,我们比较与分析每一个项目的购房人群需求,我们坚持我们大学期间所学的美学和艺术能力,只是为这些需求服务的工具,这是则灵艺术有别于其他设计公司的所在。我们的设计风格也因这些研究而持续地变化。对我们来说,做样板房设计的关键是理解居住者的生活和情感,为购房人群描绘一个美好生活的场景。

对于未来中国样板房设计发展的趋势您怎么看?会有一些转变吗?

罗玉立:随着购房人群主体向90后转移,一线都市购房人群已经越来越具备国际视野和经历,审美更趋于国际化。因此,中国的设计应该会走向更现代简约,更加艺术和舒适。

江上清风山间月

THE BREEZE BLOWING ACROSS THE RIVER, THE MOON IN THE MOUNTAINS

项目名称｜江山樾别墅样板间

设计公司｜深圳市则灵文化艺术有限公司

设 计 师｜罗玉立

项目地点｜重庆

项目面积｜350 ㎡

主要材料｜实木、金属、布艺、水晶、皮革等

摄 影 师｜曾康辉、黄书颖

设计理念｜DESIGN CONCEPT

Zest Art designed the Jiangshanyue Villa model house for the Cifi & Dowell Real Estate Development Co., Ltd extremely exuding a noble and luxurious feeling. At the same time, combined with Chongqing local characteristics, the designer created a private customized distinguished experience.

The transparent floor door not only ensures sufficient sunlight but also highlights the warm and generous life situation. The noble royal blue collides and fuses with leisurely coffee color in the space, and the grille ceiling collocating the exquisite hand-painted patterns reveal a noble flavor. The golden silk, royal blue velvet, coffee carpentry and champagne gold metal wire are unified in space strangely yet harmoniously, which is noble, generous, casual and romantic. All meet the spiritual needs of living experiences of the wealth class.

The demand of courtyard life of Chinese is originated from the taste of "And cup in hand, we talk of crops of grain." from ancient times. The courtyard life in city not only makes people enjoy times with family but also maintains the closest contact with interior space.

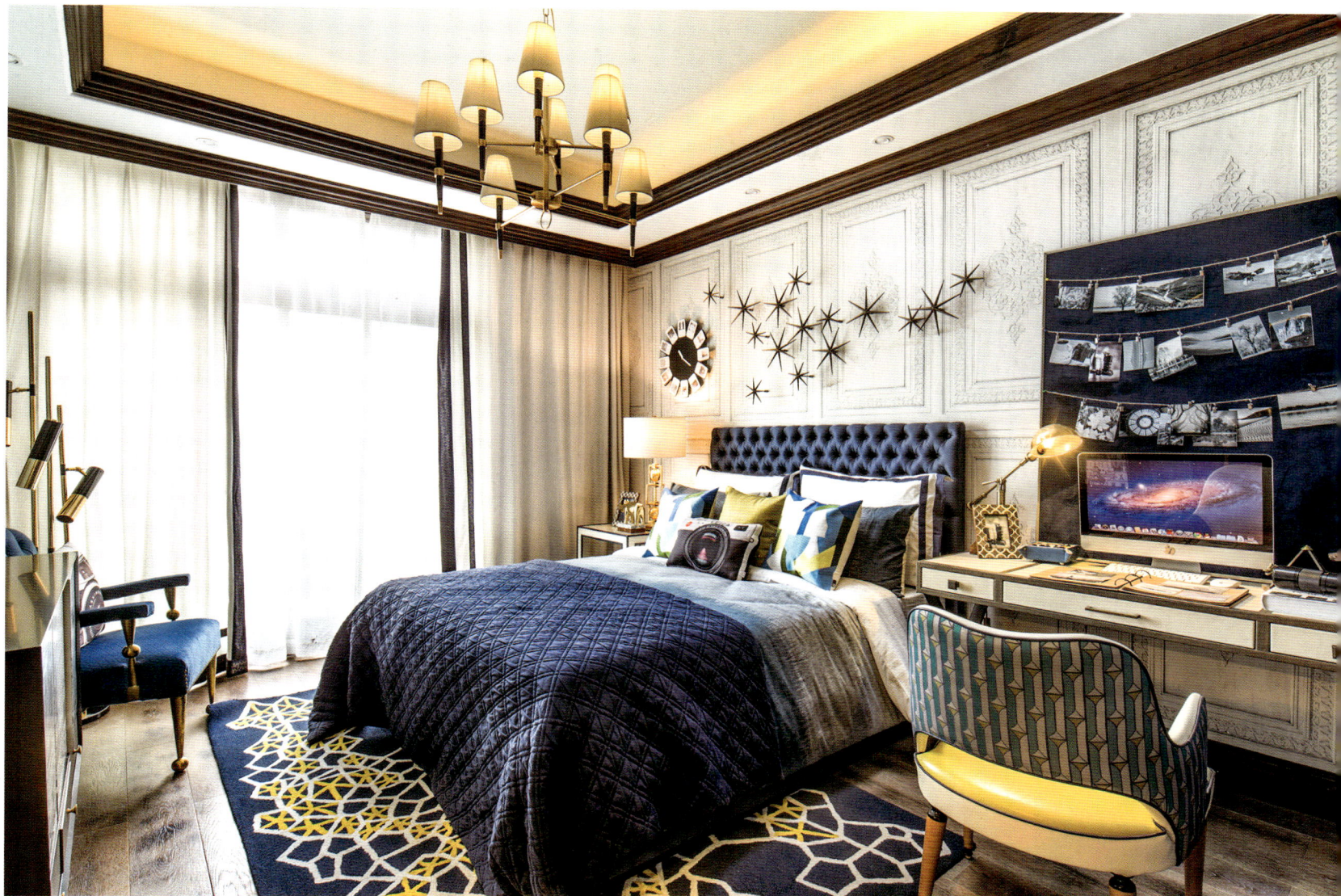

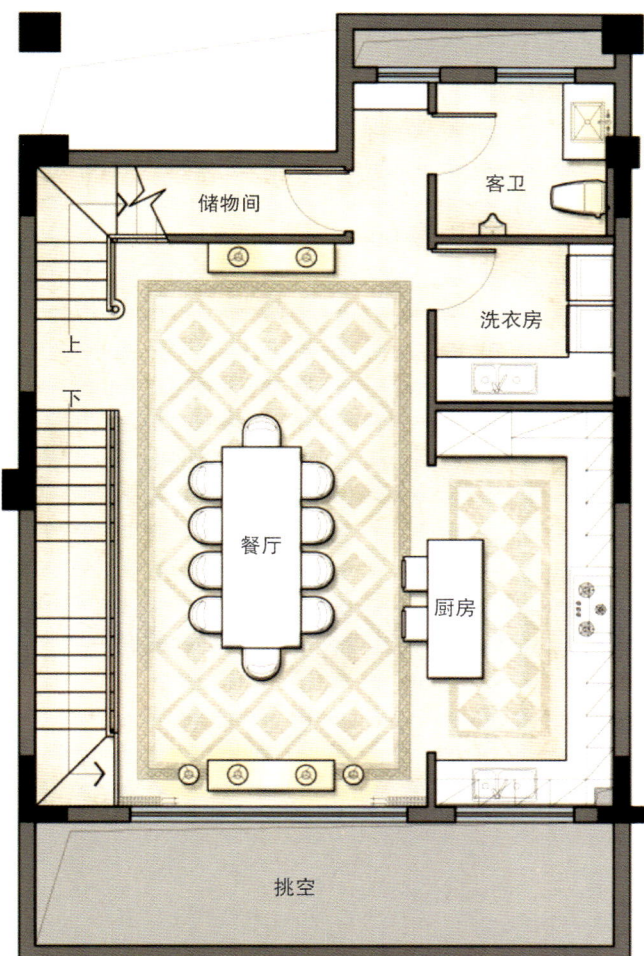

储物间

客卫

洗衣房

上
下

餐厅

厨房

挑空

　　则灵艺术为旭原创展设计的江山樾别墅样板间将高贵奢华之感发挥到极致，同时又结合重庆本地特色，打造私人订制的尊贵体验。

　　通透的落地式门户，不但保证了充足的阳光照射，更凸显了温馨大气的生活情景。贵气的宝蓝色与悠闲的咖色在空间中冲撞融合，格栅式的吊顶设计搭配精致的手绘图案，尽显贵族韵味。金色的绸缎、宝蓝色的丝绒、咖色的木作与香槟金色的金属拉丝，奇异而又和谐地统一在空间里，尊贵、大气、随性、浪漫，满足财富阶层对居住体验精神层次上的需求。

　　中国人对院落的生活诉求源于自古以来"把酒话桑麻"的情趣。城市之中的院落生活，与家人其乐融融，天伦之乐的美好也与室内空间保持着最密切的联系。

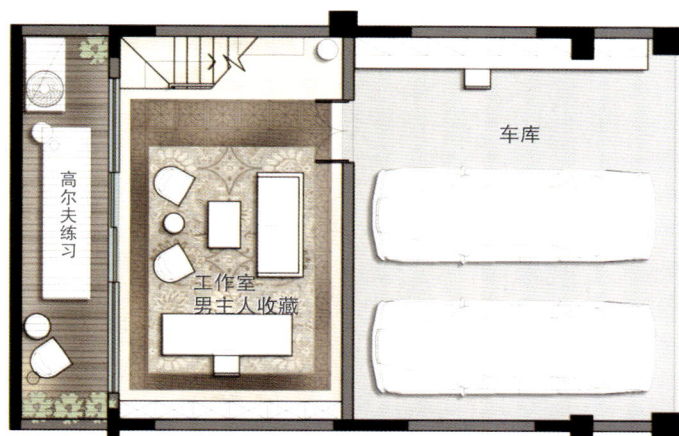

高尔夫练习

工作室
男主人收藏

车库

门厅

会客厅

挑空

庭院

客房

下沉庭院上空

露台

女孩房

走道

挑空

露台

卫生间

衣帽间

卫生间

衣帽间

男孩房

露台

主卧

挑空

露台

女主人衣帽间

主卫

RETURNING TO THE POETIC LIFE

回归生活的诗意

项目名称丨龙湖九里晴川

设计公司丨深圳市则灵文化艺术有限公司

设 计 师丨罗玉立

项目地点丨重庆

项目面积丨458 ㎡

主要材料丨实木、金属、布艺、水晶、皮革等

摄 影 师丨黄书颖

设计理念丨DESIGN CONCEPT

In a rare leisurely holiday with bright sunshine, you are preparing for the holiday bouquet for your lover on the terrace. The children downstairs are still playing, and the aged parents have returned to their room for having a break. The husband who snatches a little leisure from a busy day finally has times to wipe his beloved antiques like the children treasure the favorite toys. The time flies, and the happiness comes naturally.

The design of this case takes inspiration from the tradition, makes the beauty of life engrave in the spatial style through a transcendental and outward spiritual gesture, which every twinkle and smile is charming.

The living room retains the implicit and elegant essence of traditional Chinese style. At the same time, it represents a modern, delicate spatial characteristic. The elegant and natural tea white, the calm and tough dark coffee and the deep and winding indigo blue seem to be in the landscape and the artistic conception.

There are four bedrooms set on the second and the third floor, which each room has its characteristics. The master bedroom selects the bright and elegant colors as basic tone, and the implicit lines of furniture, delicate bedding and the carpet with abstract pattern rich of artistic atmosphere echoes with each other interestingly. By the side of the bedroom, the hostess's workspace specially set up is dominated by soft aqua; the fashionable and exquisite curve-shape furniture highlights the gentleness of women; all kinds of flower arrangements with exquisite style create a rich and exquisite atmosphere of workspace.

The theme of the boy's room is a movie series of *Star Wars*, because a 16 years old boy has a great interest in the vastness of the universe. The girl's room selects the dreamlike pink allocating with lively Tiffany blue, which is effeminate and lovely.

阳光暖暖，难得假日闲暇，你靠在露台上筹备着送给爱人的节日花束；楼下的孩子们还在嬉戏玩耍，年迈的父母已经回房午休；偷得浮生半日闲的丈夫，终于得空去擦拭心爱的古玩，犹如孩子珍视最爱的玩具。岁月如流水，幸福就是水到渠成。

本案设计从传统汲取灵感，将生活之美以一种超然物外的灵秀姿态镌刻在空间的格调之中，一张一弛春风化雨，一颦一笑皆是风情。

客厅保留了传统中式风格含蓄秀美的精髓，同时呈现出了现代、精致的空间特色。茶白的清雅自然、深咖的稳重硬朗，靛蓝的深邃蜿蜒，犹如在山水之间，意境之中。

四个卧室被设置在二层与三层，各有特色。主卧空间以淡雅色调为基调，含蓄的家具线条、精致的床品及富有艺术气息的抽象图案地毯相映成趣。旁边特别设置的女主人工作间以柔美的水绿色为主，时尚精致的曲线造型家具凸显出女性的温柔，造型讲究的各式花艺营造出丰富而精致的工作间氛围。

男孩房以《Star Wars》系列电影为主题，16岁的男孩对浩瀚的宇宙星空有着极大的兴趣。女孩房间以梦幻的粉色搭配活泼的Tiffany蓝为主，娇气而又可爱。

"After fresh rain in the mountains bare, autumn permeates evening air". The elder's room is dominated by the elegant and peaceful gray color, with the indigo blue as an embellishment. The furniture type is modern yet traditional, and the ginkgo leaf wallpaper adds exquisiteness and briskness for space.

The terrace on the third floor is the secret garden of hostess, where is an extension of the cloakroom and floral work area. The rare flowers planted carefully in the greenhouse, and the sunshine through the flowers on the flower stands projects on the wooden floor deep and shallow, which is lovely.

"空山新雨后，天气晚来秋。"老人房以清雅平和的灰调为主，以靛蓝色为点缀，家具款型现代不失传统，银杏叶的墙纸增加了空间的精致与灵动。

三层露台是女主人的秘密花园，是衣帽间和花艺工作区的延伸。花房里悉心栽种着名贵的花材，阳光透过花架上的鲜花深深浅浅投影在木质地板上，珊珊可爱。

Walking downstairs to the basement, it is a humanistic elegant space carefully designed by the designer for building the characters. Here, the owner can entertain relatives and friends, taste tea and play chess, appreciate antique, read and work, or enjoy the visual feast on the audio-video room.

"Among my guests there is no unlearned common man. In this humble room, I can enjoy playing my plainly decorated qin, or read the Buddhist Scriptures quietly". A huge landscape painting which has great originality, as well as a curioshelf with a superb collection of antique give the tea room a unique literati style of Wei and Jin Dynasties.

The basic tone of this mansion is warm and poetic. We restore the life from the style, make a painstaking investigation in the myriads of changes, and trace the essential harmonious and implicit beauty of the East. We make the "home" become an inclusive space with infinite functions and people can enjoy the life pleasantly.

　　沿梯步至地下层，是设计师精心打造的怡情养性的人文雅趣空间。户主可在此招待亲朋，或品茗对弈，或鉴赏古玩，或阅读办公，亦可到影音室享受视听盛宴。

　　"谈笑有鸿儒，往来无白丁。可以调素琴，阅金经。"一幅独具匠心的巨幅山水图，与琳琅满目的博古架一道，赋予了茶室独有的魏晋名士之风。

　　这座大宅的基调是温馨而诗意的，我们从风格中还原生活，从万千变化中抽丝剥茧，溯源东方最本质的和谐、含蓄的美感。让"家"无限放大，包罗万象，悦享生活。

高文安

香港高文安设计有限公司 创始人
深圳高文安设计有限公司 创始人

Kenneth Ko
Timeless，less is more

获得荣誉

香港室内设计之父

出版系列作品集《品鉴·品味》《品鉴·传奇》
《品鉴·悟道》等

2016年 荣膺Hall of Fame名人堂成员

2015年 入选《福布斯》中文版"中国最具影响力设计
师三十强"

2015年 与上市公司宝鹰股份结成战略同盟，出任宝鹰
集团副总裁

2014年 获IFI国际室内建筑师设计师联合会"重大国际
成就表彰"

2013年 获香港室内设计协会终身成就奖等

最好的作品，永远是下一个

THE BEST WORK IS ALWAYS
THE NEXT ONE

视界对话高文安

高老师好，您是一个比较率性的设计师，对于您的设计是怎样定位自己风格的？

高文安：我从来不会为自己设定什么风格。设计，就是为了生活，我希望出自我手的设计项目，一看就是能让人在里面安心过日子的地方。我做室内设计，不会围绕着个人的喜好，而是把重点放到客人的需求上，设计是为客人服务的，我仅是演绎他们的风格，他们的风格也就是房子的风格，我只是用自己的专业知识完美地去把客人的风格呈现出来。

那么作为一位优秀的室内设计师，有没有必要有自己个性鲜明的风格特征？

高文安： 就我自己而言，在很多人看来，我做的设计并没有什么固定的风格可言，最大的特色就是耐看，这可能也是我的风格。把三十年前设计的空间放到现在，有些材料和工艺可能过时了，但是整体的美感却不会过时。优秀的室内设计，或者说优秀的室内设计师，可以有自己的特色，但不应仅局限于某一种风格范畴，因为风格和潮流都是随时随地在变的东西，不变的是通过你个人设计作品所传达出来的品位及审美眼光，这才是设计师最应该具备的素质。我公司开了四十多年，不管是国内还是国外的客户都认"高文安"这块招牌，并不是冲着我的风格来的，而是冲着我的品位和审美来的，只要有品位和审美在，不管是任何风格、任何项目，做出来的设计都不会差。

您最近做的珠海西湖湿地别墅、海南华凯南燕湾别墅等项目，都是东南亚风格，是客户的要求还是出于对这种风格的喜爱呢？

高文安： 所有的风格都是服务于客户的，我做设计，首先强调的是服务意识。作为一个出色的室内设计师，我有自己独到的审美和眼光，也有自己擅长的设计手法，但我不会局限于某一种风格。我的设计作品里有很多是东南亚风格，这不是我个人的偏好，而是有很多客人喜欢这个风格，是客人的选择。另外，项目的所在地也比较适合这种风格，像珠海、海南都离东南亚比较近，当地气候条件相似，文化上也有很多想通的地方，客人从东南亚风格中比较容易找到情感上的共鸣，满足了今后家庭生活的需求，设计的使命也就圆满达成了。

您作为香港设计师，来内地发展的这些年中，您觉得内地设计与香港设计之间的差异化有哪些？

高文安： 2004年，我刚来大陆创立深圳分公司，能够明显感觉到内地设计和香港设计之间的差异，不管是整体设计实力与水平，还是设计的文化氛围。不过内地设计这几年突飞猛进，因为地大物博，更有百花齐放，与国际争锋的势头。地域、经济、文化的不同，必然导致内地和香港在设计上存在差异，所以我更想谈谈香港和内地的共同点。随着国力的提升，国内外对中国文化的认同感越来越高，这也促使一大批有民族特色、传统文化特色的设计在国际崭露头角，民族品牌和中国特色将会是未来内地与香港设计上的共同趋势，也会成为国际的一大潮流。

健身是您一直坚持的，对您的生活和设计有没有影响？

高文安： 从1997年一直到今天，我活得很精彩，事业顺利，人也变得更成熟，器量更大，信心更强，做人更加谦和，这一切都是健身带给我的。室内设计极其耗费脑力，坚持健身让我的身体健康保持在一个很良好的状态上，能够以饱满的精神和激情投入到设计工作中去，常常能做出让人感到惊喜的设计作品。我把设计事业作为自己的终生追求，而好的身体是实现这个追求的先决条件。我能有如今的成就，跟四十年如一日的工作是分不开的，也跟一直坚持健身是分不开的。

另外您不仅喜欢旅行，而且在世界各地都购买了一些自己的房产，是什么原因促使您在这些地方安家的？其中您最喜欢的是哪一处家呢？

高文安： 我个人是非常喜欢旅行的，从四十岁开始，三十多年里，我去过四十多个国家的上百座城市，在日本、泰国普吉岛、印尼、土耳其伊斯坦布尔、瑞士、英国伦敦等地都曾购置房产，因为我喜欢当地的文化，体验当地的生活能让我发现不一样的自己，不同的情怀会反馈到我的设计，让我的设计风格变得更加的丰满。

我对很多媒体都说过，我从来不跟我的住宅谈恋爱，我只是跟它们谈一夜情，可能几年以后我就会卖出去。我一直在变，不同的阶段有不同的生活喜好和人生感悟，而这些分布在世界各地的家就是我人生历练和沉淀的最好载体，在人生的不同时期，每一处家我都投入了十足的热情，但那只代表我的过去，不代表现在和未来，我最好的作品永远是下一个，最喜欢的也是。

最后，可以跟我们聊聊接下来您对工作和生活的安排吗？您有考虑过什么时候退休吗？

高文安： 一直以来，朋友都说我是"工作狂"，七十岁之前忙事业，全世界各地到处飞，一年到头几乎有三分之二的时间都是在飞机上。七十岁之后，可以说功成名就，我更多的是想做一些自己喜欢的，并且觉得对这个国家、这个民族有意义的事情。目前工作的重心也是以中国传统文化项目为主，比如贵州三都水族自治县和河北阜平县的古村寨改造，希望尽到自己最大的努力，让这些传统文化项目开花结果。

我没有考虑过自己具体什么时候退休，人生的舞台不要自己来写一个句号，这个句号不是你自己定的，是人家定的。只要市场尊重我、还喜欢我的作品，我就不会停下来。我停下来只有两个原因，第一是我的健康状态不允许我坚持下去，第二就是人家觉得我的作品过时了。

风情南洋 尔雅新风

INTOXICATING SOUTHEAST ASIAN STYLE WITH GRACEFUL NEW TREND

项目名称 | 珠海西湖湿地国际花园B3别墅
设计公司 | 深圳高文安设计有限公司
设 计 师 | 高文安
项目地点 | 广东珠海
项目面积 | 562 ㎡

设计理念 | DESIGN CONCEPT

In the interior design, is the natural and original Southeast Asian style must retro? It is undoubted that this mindset is not correct. This case takes modern leisure as design idea, combined with the Southeast Asian nation island characteristic and international exquisite taste. Different from the luxurious European style and placid Chinese style, the usage of the color of Southeast Asian style and the rich life taste create a romantic atmosphere.

In the foyer, the maple as "frosted autumn leaves outshine February flowers in redness" and the graceful knitted lampshade render a fiery passion and quiet. The gilded sitting Buddha statue intersperses a reassuring flavor of Zen of Southeast Asia. In the living room, Indonesian antique carved wooden doors, which closing it becomes a glimpse of the 100 years histories and opening it is a beautiful life with "as beautiful as summer flowers and autumn leaves". Double drawing rooms and the double height-empty design highlight the extravagance of the mansion. The interior decorations absorb the essence of Southeast Asian style and weaken the religious color. At the same time, it integrates the fashionable, simple and elegant modern elements which can hold the bustle in the quiet and secluded place.

In the dining room, the wood, vertical latex paint and stone texture are used mostly in facade treatment techniques. The selection of wood color, beige furniture echoes with the natural and comfortable spatial tone. Collocating the painting of Southeast Asian ethnic costumes on the wall and conch chandeliers with marine style, it creates a romantic seaside resort. In the master bedroom, designers are required to have a natural sensitive of the changes of colors so that they have enough abilities to control them.

Croci, pineapple gold and rose red is colorful yet not messy. The bold jumping colors render the vitality of space while the most usage of original woods and marble materials can exude a warm texture like a bay. The guest bedroom abandons the unnecessary decorations, which one pillow, one chandelier and one painting are enough to express a free and leisure taste of Southeast Asia. The ingenuity and interest of design are to put the life stage to the environment which can let the scenery of the lake and putting green of golf be "sneaking into the room with the wind".

餐厅，立面处理手法上多用木材、肌理漆及石材，选用木色、米白色的家具呼应自然、舒适的空间基调，搭配东南亚民族服饰做成的墙面挂画，海洋风情的海螺吊灯，营造海边度假的浪漫情调。主卧，色彩的变幻需要设计师对颜色有着天然的敏感，以及足够的功力才能驾驭。

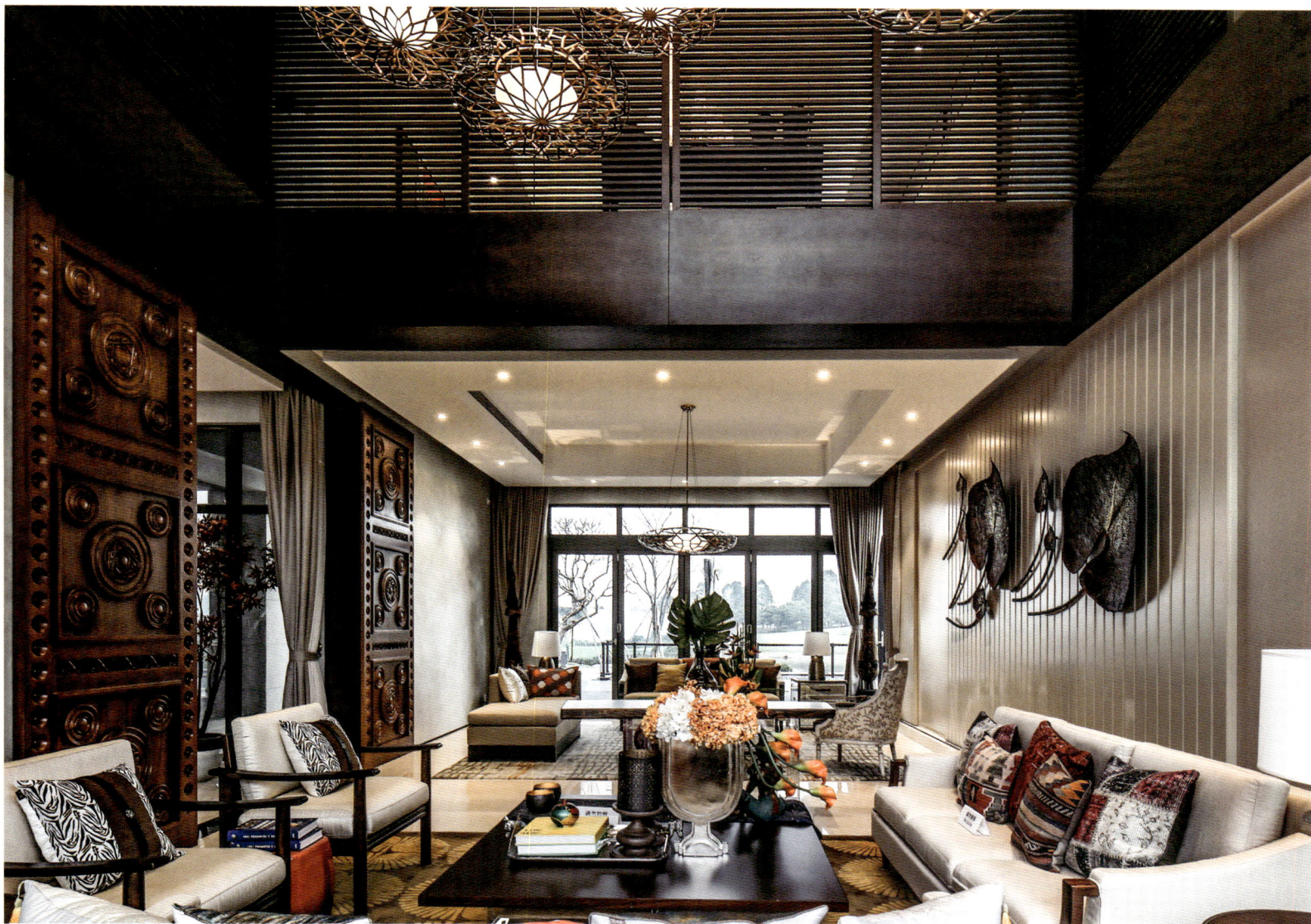

室内设计，自然原始的东南亚一定是复古的？这种思维定式无疑是不正确的。本案以现代休闲作为设计构思核心，结合东南亚民族岛屿特色及国际精致品位，不同于欧式的奢华和中式的平和，东南亚风格的用色与丰富的生活情趣更能营造浪漫氛围。

玄关，"霜叶红于二月花"的枫树，风情曼妙的编织灯罩，渲染出家的如火热情。而静谧的金身坐佛塑像，点染东南亚令人心安神宁的禅味。客厅，印尼古董雕花木门，关上是百年历史的惊鸿一瞥，推开是包容"夏花之绚烂，秋叶之静美"的秀美生活。双会客区与挑空二层的设计突显大宅的阔气，室内装饰吸取东南亚风格精髓，弱化了宗教色彩，同时融入了时尚简雅的现代元素，在清净幽谧中守住一片繁华。

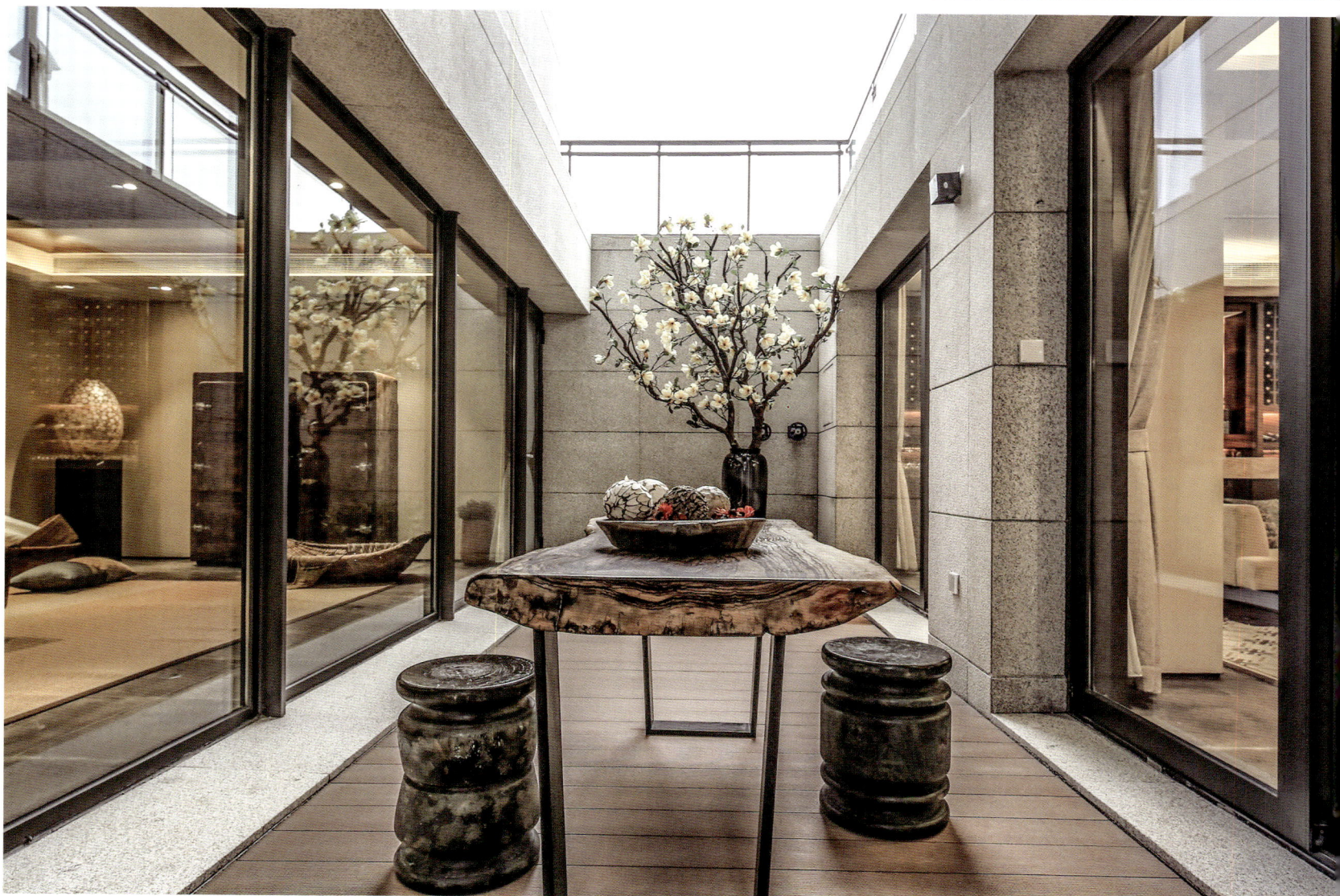

橘黄、凤梨金、蔷薇红，色彩丰富却不凌乱，大胆的跳色增添空间年轻态的活力，而原木、大理石材质的大量运用，赋予居室港湾般的温暖质感。客卧的装饰去繁从简，一个抱枕，一盏吊灯，一幅挂画，就足以晕染出东南亚的自由悠闲味道。设计的匠心和意趣是把生活的舞台交给环境，让湖景与高尔夫果岭的风光"随风潜入梦"。

The layout of the entertainment area in the basement is organized through the streamline relationship of spatial function distribution, connecting the study, gymnasium, video room and wine-tasting room which are surrounded by the lighting garden. Using the modern, simple design technique to elaborate scene, and the punchline of strong Southeast Asian color elements combining with the day light, cloud shadow and the changes of lights can create a scene in a step of Southeast Asian style.

Xihu National Wetland International Gardens is a lifestyle from luxury to plain, noisy to peaceful.

　　地下娱乐区，通过空间功能分布的流线关系来组织布局，围绕着采光花园、书房、健身房、影视室、品酒室贯穿连通，以现代简约设计手法铺陈场面，浓烈东南亚色彩的元素符号仅作为点睛之笔，结合天光云影与灯光的变化，营造出一步一景的东南亚风情。

　　西湖湿地国际花园别墅，一种从浮华走向平实、从喧闹回归宁静的生活方式。

深圳创域艺术设计有限公司
董事长、设计总监

Yin Yanming

强调创造力、秩序感及多元体验

获得荣誉

亚太酒店设计十大风云人物

《美国室内设计中文版》年度封面人物

中国最具影响力的室内设计师之一

出版个人设计专辑《设计的日与夜》《憶美》

2017年 荣膺英国SBID国际设计大奖

2017年 荣膺腾讯家居金腾奖"年度设计公益奖"

2017年 荣膺 IEED国际生态环境设计联盟"中国设计公益人物"

2016年 荣膺SIX ARTS AWARD台湾六艺奖设计爱心公益奖

2016年 荣膺IDCF DESIGN100大中华区最具影响力设计机构

2015年 荣膺"金砖奖"年度最佳别墅设计金奖等

用设计的力量，创造更多的意义与价值
USING THE POWER OF DESIGN TO CREATE MORE
SIGNIFICANCE AND VALUE

视界对话殷艳明

"设计是一门生活的艺术，是思想情感的交流，是一种想象和凝聚。它就是一个梦境之旅，每一个设计都承载着别人的愿望，但更多的是承载着自己的梦想，承载着自己对生活的感悟，对美的追求和理解，这个思维构筑的过程是我们追寻的一种自由，一种生活。"

——殷艳明

前段时间您主持并参与了一场"未来已来"中国家居发展趋势论坛，整个活动下来最大的感触是什么？

殷艳明：首次客串主持PPG大师论坛、为陈幼坚老师而来，悉心聆听受益匪浅。"随心而为""花心"两大见解独具观点，作为当代华人最具影响力的设计师，陈老师满满的干货、风趣幽默气定神闲、多元创意如数家珍。台上嘉宾们亦分别对"家""未来

家居"和"色彩"三个主题——进行解读，多元的思维在这里碰撞，共同展开对未来的探索。借用陈幼坚先生对行业属性评论的一段话与大家分享："设计的历程就如马拉松赛跑，是一条既漫长而又充满挑战性的道路。那些获奖无数的运动健将，不只单靠一副天赋的良好体魄才'上位'，亦要配合后天的悉心栽培和毅力才能达到理想的成果。设计师要成功，亦如运动健儿般，只靠天资是不够的，一个人如没有全力付出精神、时间和努力，成功是不会发生的。"

那么未来中国家居发展的趋势是什么？家居设计最应该考虑哪些因素？

殷艳明：伴随时代的发展，人们对起居生活的空间有了更高追求，未来精装房将成买房趋势，传统家装公司将淡出市场，人们更加注重人性化与个性化的设计，生活美学的理念将得到全面普及，家居中的硬装和软装搭配，是否环保，是否智能等等，设计理念的迭代正变得异常频繁。家居设计中功能与实用性是设计要解决的基本问题，我们所讲的设计人性化是在这个基础上人的内心对生活更高层次的体验和追求，它更关注人的精神方面的感受和价值观的体验。

有没有一些新的设计理念跟我们分享一下？

殷艳明：我认为未来产品设计领域和教育设计领域是值得去探索和尝试的。设计的外延是宽泛的，商业的设计领域已经有太多的关注和研究群体，也让设计定义似乎变成了商业设计的代名词，而对于设计的社会价值的挖掘还处于初始阶段。产品设计与社会大众的生活息息相关，教育与设计的结合是未来下一代提升艺术与美学教育最好的介入方式。作为设计者，我们更应该从设计的本质和体现社会价值的层面去让设计价值最大化，这也是未来的趋势。2015年我在家乡云南彝族地区走访了多所乡村小学，通过与师生的交流，结合乡村小学的现状，提出了"设计与教育相结合、用设计提升乡村教育"的公益设计理念。我们的目的不是扶贫，而是通过设计构建第三空间，为现行的教育体系作一个补充。

跟您合作这么多年，对您设计类别的繁多深感诧异，如别墅、样板房、酒店、办公、商业空间等，而且每种空间您都做得游刃有余、各具特色，您是怎样做到各类空间都能娴熟驾驭的？各类空间之间有没有什么共通性？

殷艳明：这得益于我早年在香港设计公司里接触到不同设计类别项目有关。这需要极强的综合能力，而这点也正是我们公司的优势所在。往往大型项目综合体，从外立面、酒店、公寓、住宅配套设计需要一个有体系的设计公司才可以全盘把握，大处立意，小处着眼，把人在空间中的动态感受放在第一位，注重尺度、比例，以室内建筑师的角度去诠释设计，那么不同场域的性格就会娓娓道来，收放自如了。

好像这跟您一直提倡的"多元设计"不谋而合，可以跟我们具体聊聊什么是多元设计吗？它最注重的是什么？

殷艳明：多元化是思维模式的多元，多元化思维是未来设计的发展方向。如果把设计比作横轴与纵轴两条线，在专业领域是纵向的，我们应该坚持纵向做深做精，而多元化是一种横向的发展，横向要做广，坚持多元化的发展。最近的项目是我们多元方向发展的一个尝试的探索，从商业设计、产品设计、艺术设计到公益设计项目均有涉猎。在多元时代更讲究设计策略和探索精神，我们希望在融界的设计方向走的更远。在设计与艺术相融合的时代，人文理念的挖掘和价值观已经融入到我们当下的生活状态之中，同时也是我们对于设计价值最大化的一种认知。

在我们最近的书《别墅风格大观VII》上面有您一个"龙光御海天禧别墅"的项目，是中式风格，设计手法非常成熟，出版之后，收到非常多的好评。从您一直的设计风格来看您应该是比较喜欢中式风格，而且是比较传统的中式风格，是因为您特别偏爱中国传统文化吗？

殷艳明：设计首先是商业设计，对于我个人而言也从不把自己定义为只能做某种风格类别的设计师。不断地挑战自我，不断地探索尝试，融中于西、尚古汇今，给设计赋予当代性的语言，我觉得都是好设计。最近我们做了一系列新中式、传统中式的商业题材展示空间，从我们自身的角度和视点对这个题材进行了解读和设计研究，重在抛砖引玉。如果能够以点带面，把在地性、文化性、艺术性、感性表达在设计作品里，传递出东方生活美学的情境、意境，就是对中式文化风格的致敬。

这次出版的项目也是中式风格的，对于中式设计殷老师有什么心得吗？

殷艳明：中式风格不能仅仅停留在表面语言和符号的照搬，中国文化博大精深，对于设计诠释更应该从空间的布局去探寻适合当代人居的尺度比例。从《营造法式》《营造法原》入手，把室内外空间一体化的理念作为演绎设计的方法论，以故事性、生活场景和空间美学三位一体的定义来捕捉亮点，杜绝高级折衷主义的面面俱到，最终体现设计的当代语境。

近些年新中式也一直深受大众追捧，形成一股东方设计美学的潮流，您觉得对于设计来说，什么样的设计才是潮流设计？

殷艳明：设计已经融入我们的生活，美是生活不可或缺的内在感知。未来是设计与艺术结合的大舞台，传统与创新并行，使设计融入艺术，艺术融入生活，三者自然共生。设计不是一个单一科学，它是一个应用科学，要关注的就是时代性，设计除了要了解关注文学、音乐、美术、建筑、雕塑、舞蹈、戏剧及电影这些艺术体系外，还要关注次生文化。设计归根到底是为了客户解决问题，无论简单也好、豪华也好，生活品质是必须要解决的问题，这是我们思考和存在的价值。

由此看来中国设计应该如何做到与国际接轨呢？

殷艳明：中国地域广袤，南北差异大，地域文化丰富多彩，以深圳为例，深圳是设计之都，时尚前沿的代表城市，也是设计理念和人才的聚居地。通过深圳这个窗口，我们和世界接轨，在多元化的信息时代里不断更新思维，丰富自己的设计策略。对于未来新的认知比财富更重要，那就是动力源和目标所在。学术的交流、走出去引进来、不同项目的跨国跨界合作……多种选项都是目前与国际接轨的通道，而且国内与国际的设计融合愈来愈强。设计要得到世界认同，首先要国际化，在这个基础上再融入东方精神的感召力，这是设计国际化进程里的重要开门锁。

因为经常看到您去旅游，去不同的地方走走看看，最近有没有去到一个让您印象深刻的地方？

殷艳明：前段时间去了德国、意大利、法国，也参加了米兰展，基本上每隔两年我就会去看米兰展，去感受最新的资讯和时尚潮流，了解最新的产品和设计理念，也是给自己放松和充电的机会，感受艺术的魅力和设计之美。

这些新的旅途咨讯会不会成为您设计的灵感？

殷艳明：旅行就是阅读的过程，有所得、有所想自然就有所感；换句话说行旅也是一个充电的过程，只有电力时常更新才能防止自己崩溃掉。

之前您设计的一个公益项目"卓越楼"校园改造，在我们微信公众号上面也发布过，最近获奖了，恭喜恭喜。做这个公益项目，是不是跟您本身是教师出身有关？

殷艳明：谢谢！卓域楼设计就是大家对我们公益设计理念的一个肯定的鼓励。做公益教育设计，这和我的教书经验多少有些联系，但是当年教书的工作与所学专业相去甚远，觉得不能带给孩子真正的审美教育，所以辞职进入设计公司施展自己的抱负。之后也一直有关注教育，特别是孩子，如果设计能与教育相结合，从另一个层面上带给孩子更多的关爱，让他们在设计空间里感受大千世界，这是值得持续投入和有意义的一件事。

对于设计师通过设计做公益，您怎么看？

殷艳明：设计师的职业追求是创造美，发现美，肩负着引领生活方式和重塑生活美学的责任，在另一个层面而言，我们除了帮客户做设计这一最基本的商业定义以外，我们可以反过来为社会做些事情。于我而言，一直在关注教育。设计与教育相结合，不是扶贫，而是通过第三空间为中国乡村教育作补充，提升孩子的素质教育。我们设计师可以用我们的一技之长，用我们的绵薄之力，真正做一些引发大家对教育事业的关注。当然，不能光有一个公益的心，最关键是真正做实事，能够对这个学校有真正的帮助，这一点也是大家对我的看法能够形成共鸣的地方。对于我来说，我希望用不一样的角度，不一样的方式，体现我们设计师自己能够做到，能够打动和帮助到别人的地方。

您之后还会有做公益这方面的计划吗？

殷艳明：我希望"教育与设计相结合，用设计提升教育"这个模式未来能够推广，从我们接触的学校中，大家都非常希望"第三空间"能够落地到自己的学校。但我们必须要先选择一个学校做试点，当"第三空间"完成以后，结构、功能、采光、排水，尺度关系比例，孩子喜不喜欢，如何更好地在空间内相互交流等等，这都是我们需要通过这个试点进行论证。我觉得这是有意义和有价值的事情，是真正能够弥补现行教育体制上的一些缺失，并且对于孩子未来成长是有非常大的帮助和意义的。我们的态度是坚持用设计的力量影响更多的人，明年我们的公益计划已提上日程，也希望更多的公益力量参与到我们的行动中来，践行设计与教育相结合，给乡村教育持续助力、为喜爱艺术的孩子营造一方自由天地。

月下看茶醸 烛下看海棠

APPRECIATING DIFFERENT BEAUTY FROM DIFFERENT ANGLES

项目名称 | 汕头龙光御海天禧65#联排别墅样板房

硬装设计 | 深圳创域设计有限公司

设 计 师 | 殷艳明

参与设计 | 万攀、文嘉、周燕黎、周宇达、梁深祥

项目地点 | 广东汕头

项目面积 | 720 ㎡

主要材料 | 玉石、古铜不锈钢、手绘墙纸、皮革、实木地板、艺术砖、艺术玻璃等

摄 影 师 | 张骑麟

设计理念 | DESIGN CONCEPT

In this space of 720 square meters, we try to build communications between the ancient time and modern time so that to condense scene and objects in the room. We take Chinese silk and traditional landscape culture as inspirations to build a space of depth and beauty and endow unique souls to different space.

-- Yin Yanming

As the new cultural context in modern society builds up gradually, we find that objects are not the only method of expression. The sense of aesthetic and art has turned to another dimension in the age of consumption. More and more people have noticed the importance of fulfilling their sense and emotion. In this project, designers went back to the initial point of culture aesthetic to present the pleasant relationships between human and nature smoothly, people and society as well as strings between people through fragrant and enjoyable oriental culture. Our designers intend to lead viewers to find their inner peace through this project.

Fragrant and Enjoyable Oriental Culture and Sense of Zen

Designers perfectly absorb the essence of traditional Chinese culture and position Seaward Fortune·Jade Lake Garden as a mansion of inheritance and family order. For No.65 Villa, designers distract element of color, art and forms from silk, embroidery and begonia, meanwhile, apply elements of Chinese landscape from Chinese tea culture to the interior room orders as a quality integration of neutralism and grace.

Designers apply design methods of division, transparency, combination and link. Scenes are built in multiple ways to build the sense of Zen and atmosphere in the space. In this project, nature and Chinese culture are masterly linked through the presentation of humanism interest of "Appreciate different beauty from different angles".

The living room is divided into two parts by the begonia screen. However, space is divided while the rooms are not separate. Smooth and fluent lines which link suspended ceiling and walls make the space concise. Jade stones with unique texture make the living room tender and graceful. Screen in traditional Chinese style with both tender and tough metallic outlines, dining chairs and floor with unique pattern make the dining room formal but also eased.

Peace and Graceful, Absorbed in Sense of Zen

Here are functional rooms including tearoom, family hall and a guest room on the basement one. We base our designs on inner emotion linkages from the very beginning. Frugal carpentry sketches a picture of grace and helps us find balance and beautiful memories back to the root of the culture. It's best to invite a few close friends here listening to the singing of wind, enjoying nice tea and chatting about recent fun. With linen tablecloth, glazed emerald bell-shape teacups and Pu'er tea from ancient trees, you'll find everything in the world is in tea. In this precious period, with friends from different places, we believe you'll be glad to stay a little longer here.

When it's comes to the basement two, its surrounding streamline design makes viewers feel open on the visual aspect. An audio-video room, wine-tasting room and cellar are located here and classified by their status of dynamic or static into functional rooms. Vault, collection room and other private rooms are assigned at the comparatively close cornered space. Extensive shape of the modern screen including those carefully selected elements of the landscape is applied to the corridor of a wine-tasting room through space building to present the elegant, frugal and dignified interest on aesthetic of the master.

The SPA and regimen area includes functions of massage, Khan Steam and bathtub. The room is enclosed by wooden grating walls to be harmonious to the scene of bamboo. With landscape paintings including silk parts, the room is made created peaceful and graceful with the sense of Zen for the hostess. In the flower arrangement area, designers make use of the architecture patio to build a transparent space, while the stuck-up begonia walls work in harmony with the courtyard.

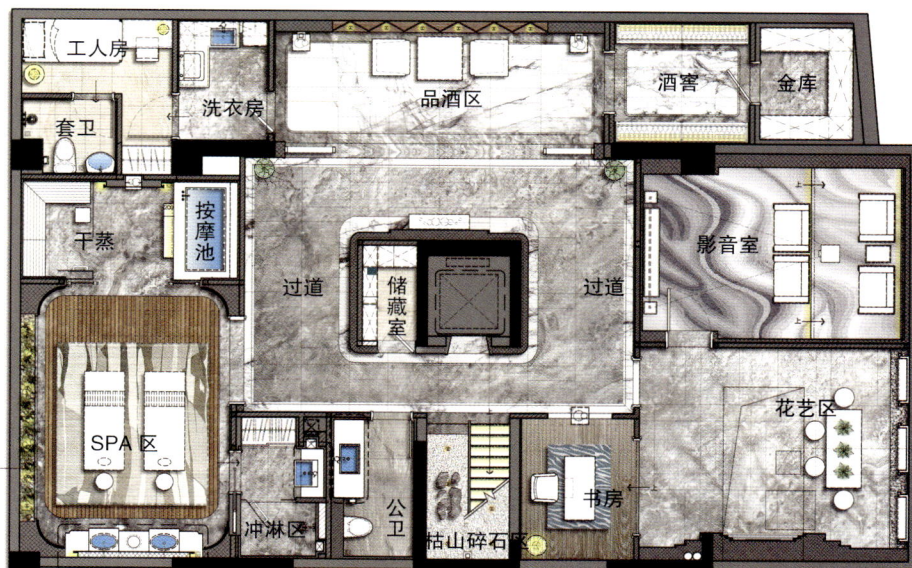

在这个720平方米的空间里，我们试图对话古今，将居室内的景、物浓缩，从中国丝绸和传统山水文化中汲取吉光片羽，打造出一个富有层次和美感的空间，让每个空间有其独特的灵魂。

——殷艳明

随着当代社会新的文化语境的体性呈现，物质并非表达的唯一方式，审美观念和艺术进入了一个消费时代的审美转向，更多的人沉迷于满足当下的感官和情感。在本项目中，设计师回到文化审美的初衷，把芳香四溢、水墨禅韵的东方主义娓娓道来，传达出人与自然、人与社会、人与人之间的美好关系，倡导人们找回内心的宁静。

芳香四溢　水墨禅韵

设计师汲取中国文化的精髓，将御海天禧·玉湖院定位为三宫制家族礼序的传世大宅；而65#别墅则从丝绸、刺绣及海棠花中提炼出色彩、艺术、形式为元素，同时，从茶文化引出中国山水挥洒在室内空间序列上，融入了更多柔和优雅的气质。

本案采用隔、透、联、通的设计手法，运用框景、借景、对景、添景等造景方式营造出空间的意境与禅味，把自然与中式文化糅合在一起，"月下看茶酿，烛下看海棠"的人文情趣在这一室之间应运而生。

客厅空间运用海棠花造景屏风一分为二，营造隔而不断的空间效果。从天花吊顶到墙面，柔顺流畅的线条变化使得空间干净利落。独特纹理的玉石，为客厅增添了不少柔美与优雅。中式屏风的雅致，配合软硬结合的金属感线条，极富质感的餐椅和特色纹案的地板，让整个餐厅在仪式感中不乏轻松和舒适。

宁静舒雅　禅意悠长

地下一层设有茶室、家庭厅、客卧等功能空间。我们的设计动作始终根植于内在的情感联系，从质朴的木器中勾勒出记忆里风雅的画面，找回平衡和文化根源的亲切记忆。在此约三两知己，听风、吟茶，聊近来的趣事，铺一匹素麻方布，几只青釉铃铛杯，一壶古树普洱，便将世味皆煮成茶。时光之里，山南水北，人生不妨停留片刻。

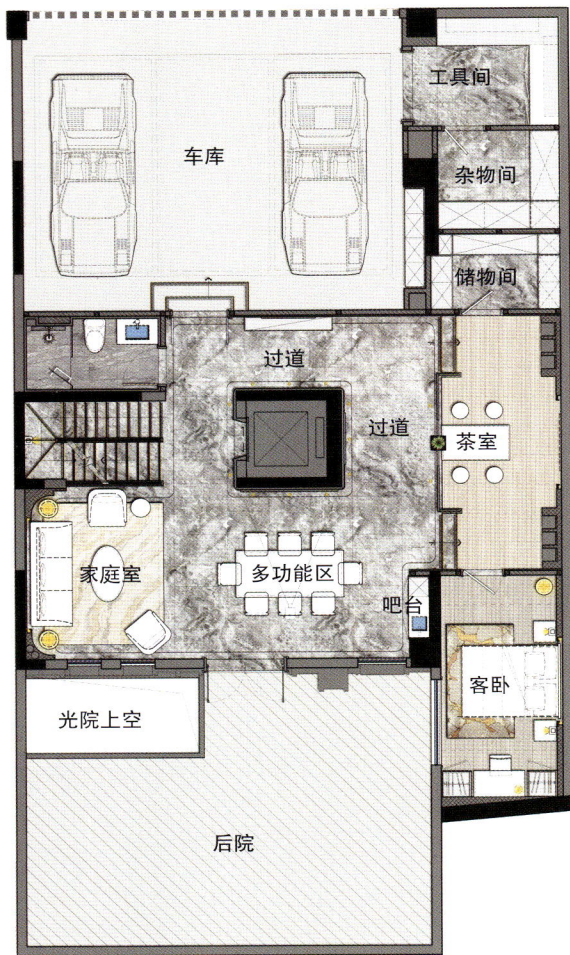

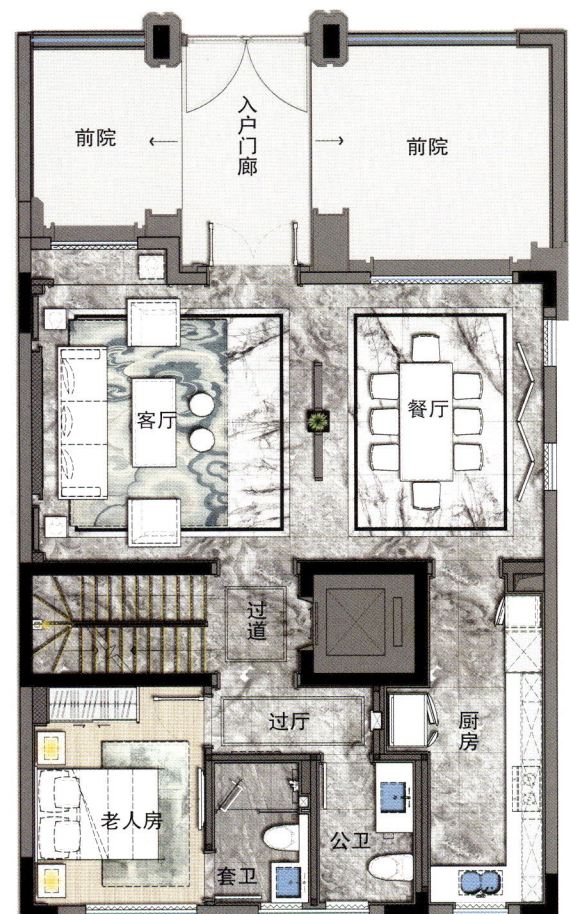

一层平面图

- 车库
- 工具间
- 杂物间
- 储物间
- 过道
- 过道
- 茶室
- 家庭室
- 多功能区
- 吧台
- 客卧
- 光院上空
- 后院

二层平面图

- 前院
- 入户门廊
- 前院
- 客厅
- 餐厅
- 过道
- 过厅
- 厨房
- 老人房
- 套卫
- 公卫

地下二层环绕式的流线设计，进入后呈现开放式的视觉感受，综合影音室、品酒区、酒窖等功能，按属性划分功能空间及动静分区。设计师在相对封闭的角落区域设置金库、收藏室这类相对私密的空间功能。品酒区走廊采用现代屏风的形体在墙体大面积铺展，提取山水元素，通过空间的营造，体现主人典雅质朴、大方端庄的审美趣味。

SPA养生区域融按摩、干蒸、湿蒸、泡池功能一体，采用木格栅墙面围合空间，与竹景相融，结合夹绢山水画，为女主人营造宁静舒雅，禅意悠长的空间意蕴。在插花区的空间里，设计师利用建筑天井为空间创造通透的气质，墙面采用海棠花叠级，与庭院氛围自然融合。

Ancient Rhyme with Innovation, Linkage of Beauty

Designers adopt the 5+1 room model for layout, which represents five suites with one guest room. This is a model which maximizes the owner's living quality and matches the living needs.

There are two suites for boy and girl on the second floor. The room for girl is embellished with pink and purple on the main wall, carpet, the chair and bedding which settle the basic tune and nature of the space. The scene, tune and light of the room have different kinds of beauty at different time in a day. Meanwhile, the theme of flower strengthens the consistency of the space through extension of the same element. The room for boy is applied alternate shapes on the walls, embroidery hanging paintings and concise tough outlines. The theme color of warm gray and highlight colors of walnut wood and blue make the whole atmosphere warm and sweet as well as energetic.

The master room is applied bronze stainless steel crafts of rigid wrap on walls and inlaid on the ceiling, art glass, leather carving and fabric. It's harsh demand for designers and construction corps behind the fantastic visual beauty. The washroom in the master room takes nature and texture representation as principles. Ice jade materials are applied on walls which have naturally extending texture as landscape paintings. Sunshine goes through vertical gratings and builds an infinite atmosphere. Distracted elements from the landscape are elaborated on the guest room walls and hanging paintings. In this room of peace, you'll feel what exactly is grand landscape and the theory in Taoism that "Man is an integral part of nature."

The tension of art comes from the unity of opposite. In this project, designers start with decoding the space to extend the value of localization. The conversation of the ancient time and modern time, the integration of softness and toughness, gracefulness and the sense of Zen are all assembled in this project.

古韵新意　美境相连

　　空间布局上，设计师采用5+1的房间模式，即五个套间加一个客卧的组合形式，最大化地提高了业主的住房需求和居住品质。

　　二层分别设置男孩和女孩两个套房。女孩房使用粉色、紫色点缀在主墙、地毯、单椅、床品上，奠定了整个空间的基调与属性，空间里的每一个景、每一个色调、每一个灯光在不同时分都有一种不同的美。同时以花朵为主题，通过相同元素的延伸，增强了空间的连贯性。男孩房的墙体则运用形体的穿插，刺绣艺术挂画及简洁硬朗的线条呈现，暖灰色的空间主色调结合胡桃木色及蓝色的跳色使整个氛围温馨而不失活力。

　　主卧结合墙身硬包、天花嵌入的古铜不锈钢、艺术玻璃、皮雕和布艺，绝佳视觉美的背后其实是对设计师和施工团队的严苛高要求。主卫以自然、质感呈现为主要法则，墙身采用冰玉石材，纹理如水墨般自然延展，日光透过竖向格栅，营造出无限的意境氛围感。客卧采集山水元素铺陈在墙面、挂画上，在这个沉静的空间里，感受烟波浩渺，天人合一的悠远意境。

　　艺术的张力来自于对立统一。在此项目中，设计师从空间解读入手，把本土化特性的价值加以延伸，古与今的对话、软与硬的结合、优雅与禅意都在此交融。

CAC卡纳设计
创办人暨首席执行设计师

张炜伦

Karen Chang

致力突破风格的限制，探索文化的边界，寻求人与空间灵性上的契合

获得荣誉

2017年 APDC亚太室内设计精英邀请赛酒店空间大奖

2017年 APIDA酒店空间铜奖

2017年 金外滩奖 最佳售楼处空间奖

2017年 艾特奖 最佳陈设艺术奖

2015年 APDC亚太室内设计精英邀请赛 样板房类银奖

2015年 APDC亚太室内设计精英邀请赛 样板房类佳作奖

2014年 APDC亚太室内设计精英邀请赛 样板房类金奖

2014年 APDC亚太室内设计精英邀请赛 样板房类佳作奖等

探究人与空间关系的适切性

EXPLORING THE APPROPRIATENESS OF THE RELATIONSHIP
BETWEEN HUMAN AND SPACE

视界对话张炜伦

张老师您好！首先非常感谢您参加我们的访谈。您在1999年创立了卡纳设计，至今已有19年，做过各种空间的设计，您在进行空间设计前的思考是什么？思考的核心是什么？

张炜伦：进行空间设计前，除了考量人与空间关系的适切性，还包含空间塑形以及与文化、与建筑的融合感、收放比例关系、细节把控等众多设计的考量。在每一个项目里面，每一个区域的比例是不同的，不应该从不一样的设计理念出发，而是对整个空间进行一个系统的整理，从一个概念到手法的植入应是相同的，这样空间的完整度才会贯穿一体。

曾经经手一个售楼会所的案子，项目空间本身是叠墅，需要把叠墅打造成高级售楼会所。在现有格局不变动的情况下，如何呈现空间的最大功能性？营造一个兼具商业洽谈空间的氛围和会所功能的同时，如何布局才能支持日后业主对空间循环再利用？这便是围绕此次项目设计概念的主要思考切入点，也是进行空间设计前的思考核心。最终呈现规整格局下空间的延伸性，并试着将功能性做到保留。

您强调人与空间的适切性，人在怎么样的空间里会获得舒适感？又是如何去感受空间里的比例关系呢？

张炜伦： 人在一个空间里面只有体验到尺度和整体的感觉，才能把空间的印象深深地留在记忆里。而设计师则需将所学习、体会、经历过的文化精神，调整并实践，使之融接于每个当代的空间需求里。

例如将现代开窗形态结合中式比例关系来呈现空间的舒适感。结合室内与室外景观的关系调整开窗面，突显自然光线之美。把建筑的比例应用到室内，于踢脚线而言，不像极简风格那么锐利，也不用像欧式古典风格那么繁复，恰到好处的3~5厘米，这样的比例还应用到室内吊顶的收边、色彩的收边，甚至于每一个小的细节。同时，通过设计与文化的完美融合来增加环境的人文气息和体验价值。

中式的比例关系把握好后，即使空间里没有很特殊的中式语汇，也还是能让人们感受到一股扑面而来的中式美感和中式氛围。这些都是古老中式文化、中式美感在设计中的改进、提炼、再运用。

那么人与空间关系的适切性，落实在具体的哪些方面？

张炜伦： 首先，这要回归到空间塑形中，什么是我们设计想表达的，而不是表面上需要什么材质或是风格。这样的设计不容易过时，因为它回归的不是流于形式的流行。

其次，讲究室内与建筑有融合感，这是设计上的主轴之一。室内设计不可能跟建筑完全违和，让室内外的感觉有一致性，提升了项目的完整度才会成功。

关于细节把控。我觉得细节是非常重要的，细节如果跟大的框架、精神没有统一，就没有办法把设计精神完整地传达出来，就会变得似像非像。

另外，要把握好适切性，前期平面图和实体空间的关系需是一致的。设计师送来的每一个项目图纸，团队都会进行多次调整，比如家具的比例、家具的数量。因为只有平面是对的，现场的空间关系才会对，不然即便陈设物件再漂亮，到现场摆设时也会给人不适切的感觉。

长期合作下来可以发现，您作品的用色很得人心，以《海月甲第》为例跟我们分享一下，在配色和材质方面您有什么独到见解？

张炜伦： 这个项目是新中式风格，想呈现的是融合一些中式元素的现代空间，此后再搭配中式和现代结合的色彩。因为我们生活在现代，我们的建筑不是古建筑，为了实现建筑内在与外在的和谐一致，室内设计部分也不宜过于中式。设计上所需要呈现的中国文化，则采用比较隐晦的方式，使用中式的比例关系、具有明暗对比的色彩、合适的软装饰来营造一个比较中式的空间氛围。

色彩是《海月甲第》项目的突破所在。硬装采用米色与高级灰，又用蓝色作为对比。结合2017年时尚界最流行的色调，将灰、蓝之间的层次搭配感营造于室内空间中。将法式风格融入中式的建筑中，用一种对比的手法营造空间艺术。

该项目特意缩减木饰面的比例，代之以烤漆面处理，同时金属收边的运用、低调的古铜拉丝材质，勾勒天花板以及家具的干练气质，在细节上更具有现代质感。

卡纳设计做的《湘湖壹号》做好当天就出售了，您是如何平衡一个住宅项目的宜居性与商业性的？

张炜伦： 面对不同项目会有不同的呈现手法。设计最初对空间的思考重点是平衡，其中对环境和设计整体结构的考量、对动线如何流畅地贯穿于室内空间的把控，以及对材质的选择，都是设计中所需要平衡之处。

《湘湖壹号》是将东方奢雅气韵低调融入华丽古典元素，注重动线流畅性的同时，巧妙地将空间型态与商业型态结合，在色彩和材质搭配上做了大胆的创新，让功能与美感兼备，蓝色、白色、灰色的主基调搭配大理石墙面，以各种金属元素区别于商业空间的材质选择，用来提升整个房间的格调，从而达到一种宜居性与商业性的平衡。

您认为设计师如何处理好住户与空间、设计师与甲方的关系？

张炜伦： 首先是平衡居住者与空间的关系。

我们曾设计一处养老项目，在设计过程中就以着力考量设计之外的综合能力来平衡居住者与空间的关系。例如设计师为保证空间的规整，将楼梯隐于接待台后方，格局舒爽，这也符合了老人多使用电梯的生活习惯；考虑到过于明亮的光线会让老人产生刺目之感，我们特意将顶部吊顶做得较为封闭，让自然光线借由侧面穿过，既保证照明又不会让阳光毫无遮拦。

在设计师看来，情境的营造远甚于细节本身。我们在长者居家生活的细节中演绎作品，注重温度与人、与空间和时间的关系，温度代表有感情，有感情的设计就是恰到好处，这也是一种人文情怀的展现。

张炜伦

Karen Chang

致力突破风格的限制，探索文化的边界，寻求人与空间灵性上的契合

其次，要平衡设计与甲方的关系。

每个项目都有它们的不同点，我们所注重的还是围绕空间本身去跟甲方做沟通。过程中我们会在设计方案中的考量与甲方所考虑的问题之间进行平衡取舍，将双方的观点进行筛选、糅合。

一般在项目前期我们会建议怎么样的空间平面才是好的，而甲方也会从他们的立场出发提出他们的观点，这期间的沟通是比较多的。但在项目的后期，我们会稍坚持一些，比如项目用材、空间功能性等，或是在室内设计的比例问题上会特别斟酌，因为项目执行是作品最终效果呈现的关键。

最后，是要平衡室内设计与建筑设计的关系。

在与建筑师合作室内项目时，理念上会有很多需要互相磨合的地方。以开窗方式为例，在室内的规划上我们可能建议将窗户分五块，每部分都需要大面积开窗，而建筑师会觉得这个开窗面积在比例上与其他地方不够协调，那我们就会再继续讨论，直到最终共同完成建筑与室内相和谐的空间。

卡纳设计现有100多人，在公司团队建设方面，您怎么看？

张炜伦：如同前面的分享，作为设计师无论是设计还是公司的管理，对我来说都是一种对于空间的思考态度。面对设计，思考的是人与空间的适切性，而面对公司，则会思考人在卡纳团队的发展空间、上升空间。空间本身有各自的目的，但无法自发地产生意义，而当空间里置放了人与思维，那么空间便会酝酿出属于这个场域里独特的气质与生命力。

宁静致远 淡泊明志

A QUIET AND TRANQUIL VILLA WITH ELEGANT TEMPERAMENT

项目名称 | 海月甲第　　　　项目地点 | 浙江宁波

设计公司 | 卡纳设计　　　　项目面积 | 462 ㎡

设 计 师 | 张炜伦

设计理念 | DESIGN CONCEPT

The designer selected the jade, marble and oak as veneer, and tried to construct the Chinese reputable family style from the view of contemporary. The design of functional division contains both collection and smooth construction line functions. At the same time, the designer rebuilt the window of the building to introduce the scenery of courtyard which not only can achieve the purpose of view borrowing but also expand the spatial pattern.

The master bedroom is focused on hard linen pack, herringbone parquet wood floor and floral wallpaper showing a traditional image to add a remote, quiet, reserved and elegant atmosphere for space. The abstract painting with wide range at the head of bed makes space full of tension, and the champagne gold color allocating with gold materials make the overall temperament generous and fashionable.

In the basement, the gray color echoes with dead wood and flowers, and the furnishings of tea table, the placing of pen and paper on the desk, and so on, all of these create a quiet, quaint and antique cultural atmosphere. Here, the tea-tasting room, chess room, painting room, collection room and other functional areas are arranged in order, interpreting the elegant living interests of the owner.

The whole design uses concise but abstract elements to continue the succinct technique and the gray color can maintain the integrity of visual and spirit.

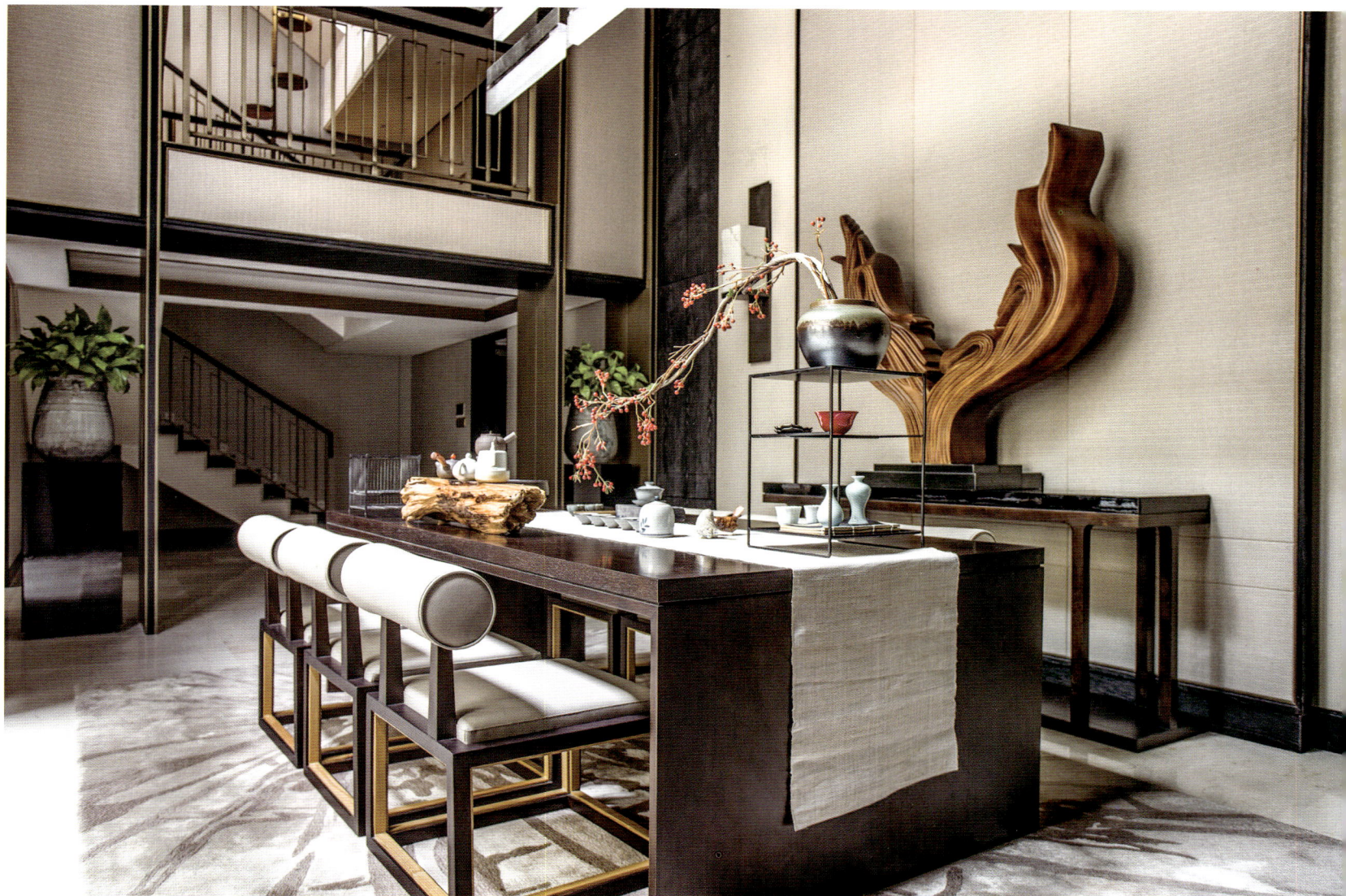

　　本案设计师甄选玉石、大理石、橡木饰面等，力图构筑出当下视野的中式望族风范。功能分区设计兼顾收纳与流畅动线。与此同时设计师改造了建筑的开窗面，引入庭院风光，既达到借景的目的，也拓展了空间格局。

　　主卧空间以麻布硬包、人字拼木地板、暗花壁纸寄予传统意象为主，增添空间幽远宁静、含蓄高雅的气氛。床头大跨度的抽象画赋予空间十足的张力，香槟金搭配金属元素，使得整体气质既大气又时尚。

　　地下室中灰色调与枯枝插花等元素相互映衬，桌前茶席的摆设、案台纸笔的铺陈等等，都给空间营造出宁静祥和、古香古色的文化氛围。这里品茗、对弈、泼墨、收藏等功能分区排列有序，无不诠释着业主高雅的生活志趣。

　　设计整体以简练而抽象的元素延续洗练笔法，灰色调一脉相承以保持视觉和气韵的完整性。

凌子达

KLID达观国际设计事务所
设计总监

Kris Lin
以豁达的胸襟看世界，开阔的视
野带来新的创意与想法

获得荣誉

自2008年以来，已获300多项国际设计类大奖：

荣获德国红点（REDDOT）工业设计领域大奖，共4项

荣获德国IF设计大奖，共6项

连续7年获得意大利A'DESIGN大奖，共36项

连续4次获"设计界奥斯卡奖"之称的
英国安德马丁（ANDREW MARTIN）国际室内设计大奖

连续3年荣获英国伦敦FX国际室内设计奖年度大奖，其中
2次获得年度最高奖WINNER

连续6年荣获英国伦敦SBID国际室内设计大奖，共12项奖

连续7年荣获美国ID杂志BEST OF YEAR室内设计大奖，
共8项大奖

连续5年荣获美国洛杉矶INTERNATIONAL DESIGN大奖
的28项大奖，其中6项金奖

连续4年荣获德国设计大奖，共25项等

做自己想要的设计
DOING THE DESIGN WHAT YOU WANT

视界对话凌子达

凡是您设计的作品几乎都能得到大家的认可，成为年轻设计师们学习、模仿的对象，能跟我们分享一下您是如何获取设计灵感的吗？

凌子达：我觉得灵感是来源于生活的，就像上海建发展示中心（Skynet）这个项目，它的设计灵感就来源于渔民赖以生存的渔网。我们将顶面与四面墙连在一起，合二为一，仿佛一张渔网被抛洒至水面的一瞬间，渔网线条被充分延伸形成一个交织纹路空间，展现出每根线条连结的光滑流畅与优雅。在施工中，我们运用了中国传统建筑工艺中的榫接技巧串连着天网，为空间创作上创造出富有视觉艺术的效果。

我们也知道，您比较少在网上宣传自己设计的项目，但前段时间您设计的办公室因为一部热门电视剧火了一把，对此您怎么看？

凌子达：《欢乐颂》的电视剧组有一个采景部门，专门关注新的楼盘、建筑、景点，到处采景，并对景点做定位。他们对小包总的定位是年轻、有品味的总裁，于是找到了我们办公室。有很多剧组都来找过我们，但我们只是有选择性地承接了一部分。除了《欢乐颂》，我们办公室还拍了吴奇隆主演的连续剧。因为设计比较现代，所以定位一般是年轻的总裁。很荣幸受到《欢乐颂》剧组的青睐，也希望更多的人会喜欢我们的作品。

您的室内设计风格多以新中式为主，您为什么会对中式风格情有独钟？在您看来，做新中式风格的精髓是什么？

凌子达：中式设计风格体现东方独有的特点，可以表达的方式也很多。中式风格可以给人安定、舒适、惬意的感觉，这种环境会让人感觉很放松，不会很紧张很压抑。我们对新东方的诠释是：既现代又禅意。

像之前我们设计的南京证大九间堂别墅样板房，是新东方风格。在整体空间上，利用得天独厚的自然景观，结合桃花源记中的桃花、鹅卵石和栅格纹路等东方元素设计，因地制宜，创造如诗如画的舒适意境，给居住者带来心灵的安抚。将这些作为空间上的规划理念，表达出设计师对于安定与幸福生活的无限追求。

在我看来新中式风格的精髓是把古典元素巧妙地融入现代设计中，给人以清新、不拘一格的全新感受。

长期合作下来，我们发现，您在许多项目中都用到一个梅花图案，这个图案有什么特别的含义？

凌子达：“梅花香自苦寒来”，我个人是比较喜欢梅花的气节。艺术的表达有时并不一定要有某种特殊的含义，运用某个图案或装饰都是设计师自己凭感觉去运用的。

以往的采访中您多次提到“太极”，您初次认识“太极”是什么时候？能告诉我们您对它如此钟爱的渊源吗？

凌子达：“太极”一词源于《周易》，是中国传统文化上道家的哲学思想，代表宇宙万物间的一种秩序状态。

中国古人经过长时间对各种自然现象的观察，认识到宇宙间的一切事物都存在着对立与融合的两面，即“阴”和“阳”，其意指天地间的一切事物和现象都包含着阴和阳，以及表与里的两面，也代表着宇宙的天和地，而它们之间是既互相对立又相互和谐存在的关系。这即是物质世界的定律，是众多事物的纲领和由来。

在建筑的立面设计上我会分两个体块，一个深色，一个浅色，分别代表了太极中“阴”和“阳”两个元素，这两个体块互相对立而又相互和谐存在，以融合的方式形成一个完整的个体。我很喜欢太极中融合的概念。

除了新中式，您有没有想过尝试更多其他的住宅设计风格？为什么？

凌子达：其实我们的设计是根据甲方的需要来呈现的，根据不同的楼盘、样板房等，我们会提出不同的设计方案。当然除了新中式，我们也会做其他风格的设计，但我们设计的宗旨是我们的客户一定要是发自内心地喜欢我们的作品，而不是来找我们做一个项目就结束了，那样的话就没什么意义了。目前我们也在着手开发国外的项目，设计风格也会有所不同。

众所周知，您获得众多国内外的设计大奖，在办公室专门有一面“证书墙”，您会建议年轻设计师多参加设计比赛吗？

凌子达：参赛是鼓励自己的方式，但比赛有很多可能性，一定要保持一颗平常心。

您创立了达观设计事务所，达观设计事务所成立初期是凭借什么在上海这个大都市站稳脚跟的？

凌子达：达观国际设计事务所始于台北，2001年来到上海，至今已经16年了，现阶段仍在发展当中，目前以设计事务所的方向经营，公司所有的项目都是自己主创。公司架构很简单，有50几人，每个项目都坚持自己做主创，再配2~3个设计师。这样的模式会引领公司向好的方向发展，特别是项目量的限制，我们每年接的项目都有固定的数量。

对达观来说，作品很重要，我们对项目的定义是，它可以成为年度作品，或是成为不同领域的新作品代表。达观的核心价值是“设计创新”，设计的关键在于主创，目前主创是我们做主控的。我们在国内最主要的项目在以上海为中心的长三角，及深圳、广州、厦门。很多时候我们要坚持自己的风格，但在这个过程中受诸多因素的限制也要放弃很多。

在公司管理方面，您参与得多吗？在采访的最后，能否跟我们分享一下您经营事务所的一些成功经验，给我们年轻的设计团队一些建议？

凌子达：在设计公司的经营上，主要是我们主控创作的。这种模式容易出好作品，但是也很累，因为所有项目都要亲力亲为，要做项目方案汇报、深化汇报等，都需要我们亲自去对接甲方。我觉得创业就是不要怕苦、怕累还有加班，做工作室会很辛苦。深圳、广州、香港的很多设计师事务所在成功获得一定知名度后，往往会转型为企业，而原先的创始人退居二线。但台湾的设计事务所一般都会一直把自己放在第一线，其公司也往往带有个人风格，达观就有自己的风格。

达观设计在上海的16年里经历了很多，但我们一直坚持自己的风格，不是有项目就接，也不是预算高就接，我们曾经放弃过很多案子。有时我们在意这个案子是不是我们真正想做的，或者这个案子可以给我们多少空间，而不是有多高的利润，这些都很重要。

THE DECENT URBAN ROMANCE

婉转的都市浪漫

项目名称 | 上海旭辉铂悦滨江别墅A户型
设计公司 | 达观设计
设 计 师 | 凌子达
项目面积 | 230 ㎡

设计理念 | DESIGN CONCEPT

The overall style is modern French style, integrating the classic spirit into the whole design, such as symmetry, axis, etc., also including the classical frame and door pocket. The designer wanted to make some breakthroughs in the classical design concept, so he created some new ideas on the presenting elements. In the design, the wall panel is still in European style but simplifying the classical lines, using some modern materials like stainless steel materials to outline the panel lines, which not only can contain the classical elements but also can present a sense of modern.

The designer also made some innovations on parquet on the ground. Instead of the traditional wave wire technique, the petaline elements are used as the parquet on the ground for creating a creative, low-key and luxurious parquet effect.

The light color is selected as the overall interior soft decoration color tone, presenting a romantic style. All the furniture are from famous brands, and the sofa adopts the white leather material. The elegant visual enjoyment makes soft and hard decoration interact with each other.

整体是现代法式风格，把古典的精神都融入整个设计中，如对称、轴线等，包括古典线板和门套的做法。想在古典的设计理念上做一些突破，所以在呈现的元素上做一些新的想法。在设计中，墙面的护墙板还是用欧式的做法，但简化了古典的线条，用一些现代的材料，如不锈钢的材质来勾勒出护墙板的线条，让古典元素不流失的同时也有一种现代感的展现。

在地面的拼花上也做了一些新的创新，不是传统的波打线的手法，而是创造出有创意的也富含低调奢华的拼花效果，所以用花瓣的元素来做地面的拼花。

整体的室内软装色调是浅色系的为主，呈现一种浪漫的温度，在家具的部分都用知名品牌，沙发都是采用白色真皮。高雅的视觉享受，让软装与硬装也是交互辉映着。

The whole villa contains one basement and three floors, so the elevator is used for communicating with four floors. The basement is used for family activities and entertainment, setting a bar area, living room, billiards room and other areas in an open design technique mainly. The first floor contains the living room, dining room, kitchen and afternoon tea parlor. The second floor is based on the elder's room and children's room. The third floor is master bedroom with independent cloakroom and restroom, which can reflect the positioning of high-end customers.

Besides, there is a small loft space which is a family activity room including a parent-child activity area and a children's entertainment area.

　　整套别墅有三层地上的空间，带一层地下室，四层空间用电梯来联通。地下一层用于家庭活动和娱乐活动，设置吧台、起居厅、运动台球室等空间，以开放式的设计手法为主。一层空间是客厅、餐厅、厨房以及下午茶的会客厅。二层是父母房和儿童房为主。三楼是主卧室，从独立的衣帽间和卫生间中也能反应出高端客户的定位。

　　另外有一个小小的阁楼空间，定位是家庭的活动室，有亲子的活动区、小孩的娱乐区。

史迪威

上海元柏建筑设计事务所 总经理
上海元展建筑室内设计事务所 总经理

Steve. Shih
以人为本

获得荣誉

上海交通大学 客座教授

2016年 艾特奖 最佳样板房设计 入围奖2项

2016年 中国室内设计二十年总评榜
最具创新设计机构

2016年 中国室内设计二十年总评榜
中国室内设计优秀成就奖等

在市场中成就自我
ACCOMPLISHING MYSELF IN THE MARKET

视界对话史迪威

史老师您好！非常感谢您在百忙之中参加我们的访谈。我们都知道您毕业于美国哈佛大学建筑设计研究所，是学建筑设计出身的，跟我们分享一下做建筑设计与室内设计的不同体验？

史迪威： 首先建筑是室内的框架，而室内则是建筑的延伸。建筑设计侧重于外观与室内房间，室内设计更重视材质、家具等各种软装的结合。

室内设计是一项复杂且涉及面广的工作，您能跟我们分享一下您在做室内设计时最注重的是什么吗？

史迪威： 室内的空间与格局是我设计的重点，室内是空间建筑，它着重于空间的安排、动线的流动、灯光的处理和材质的搭配等。

您坚持"以人为本"的设计理念，以人为本的具体表现有哪些？

史迪威：人本的理念其实是就居住空间而言的，主要考虑人体工学、动作安排、空间层次、收纳储藏、人员互动空间和瞬间弹性变化等等。

我们了解到，您的孩子跟您一样学设计，作为长辈，在您看来，新一代设计师的设计观念跟从前有什么不一样吗？

史迪威：他们学习的手法更前卫，更重视外形与吸引力，也更重视当下的流行趋势与风格，而我会更重视设计的本质与平面。新一代设计观念着重有形表现，传统的设计观念更重视空间的安排，这并不对立，它们是相辅相成的。

设计师群体在成长，室内设计这个行业也在成长。国内的室内设计行业发展日新月异，在您看来，目前国内的室内设计水平发展到了哪个阶段？

史迪威：从整个市场来看，国内设计水平进步很快，目前比较受欢迎的现代风、工业风都与国外接轨了，而具有本土文化特色的新中式风格更是得到国内外的一致称赞，越来越受到新一代人的青睐。

那么在您看来，国内室内设计目前的发展阶段有哪些明显的短板？

史迪威：目前国内设计的发展主要表现是设计风格不够多样化，其次是个性化不足，其深厚内敛的文化底蕴得不到充分展现，但这些都在市场的需求与发展中快速地完善与进步。

史老师您在国外也有许多设计作品，在您看来，国内室内设计跟国外的相比，有哪些比较明显的不同？

史迪威：国外有国外的市场，国外的住宅设计在形式上更简约，更多地运用一些特殊材料，而项目空间也偏平实，3D、4D造型的设计更受欢迎。

由此看来，您觉得，国内外室内设计存在这些差异主要有哪些方面的原因？

史迪威：产生这些差异的原因是多方面的，不能以单一的视角去分析。宽泛地说，我认为原因在于教育方式、方法不同，经济发展的轨迹不同，往细里看也在于业主的取向不同、对设计师及其方案的尊重程度不同等等。另外，设计团队与材料商的配合也是造成这些差异的原因之一。

我们都知道，现在还有很多年轻的台湾设计师、设计团队到内陆来发展，事业起步时不免会遇到许多困难，您有什么建议给他们吗？

史迪威：国内设计界的进步与竞争都是非常快速和激烈的，同时内陆幅员辽阔、区域文化不同，对于已经形成一定风格特点的台湾设计团队而言，进入内陆发展必须保持学习的态度、积极的精神，还要有坚强的毅力和持久的力量去完成最好的作品。另外，还要学会与客户交朋友，不好高骛远、不按部就班，团结队伍往成功的方向努力。

A ROMANTIC FEELING IN THE POST-INDUSTRIAL ERA

后工业时代的浪漫情怀

项目名称丨上海精文香水湾（御湖别墅）

设计公司丨上海元柏建筑设计事务所

项目面积丨778 ㎡

设计理念 | DESIGN CONCEPT

From conciseness to complexity, and whole to part, the crafted design of this case with gold and flower pattern inlay shows a precise impression. It retains the general style of materials and colors which can make people feel the traditional historical traces and vigorous cultural deposits. On the other hand, it abandons the complex texture and decorations and simplifies the lines. This case combines the nostalgic, romantic feelings with the demands of modern life which is luxurious, elegant and fashionable to reflect the personalized aesthetic views and cultural taste of the post-industrial era.

The designer combines the fayer of entrance on the first floor with elevator hall to form a series of combining life tracks composed of piano room, bar, the western restaurant, breakfast room and the family

room. On the second floor, the access to stairs and elevator forms a pattern of the double master bedroom, adding the image of a cultural art gallery and height-raised living room. Each bathroom of the master bedroom has its characteristic, which adds quite a few interests of the bedroom.

The outdoor courtyard is connected from the barbecue area of the dining room on the first floor of the garden in the basement to form a complete outdoor life, achieving the best effect of mutual echoing by indoor and outdoor arrangements. The basement is fully integrated with the sunken garden, highlighting the spatial richness of the study, billiards room, SPA area, bar, wine cellar, etc.

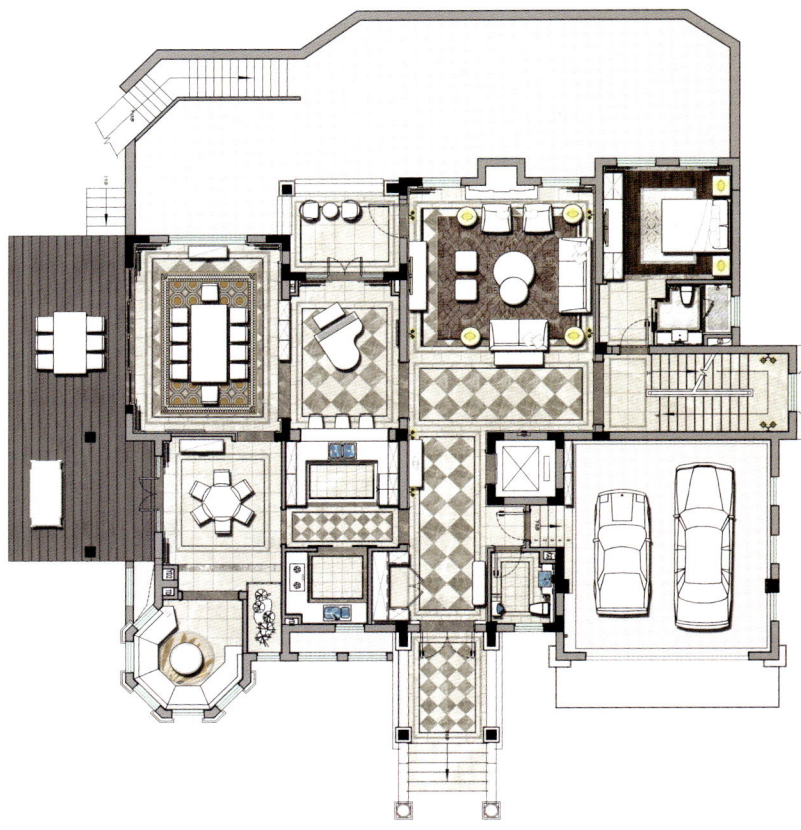

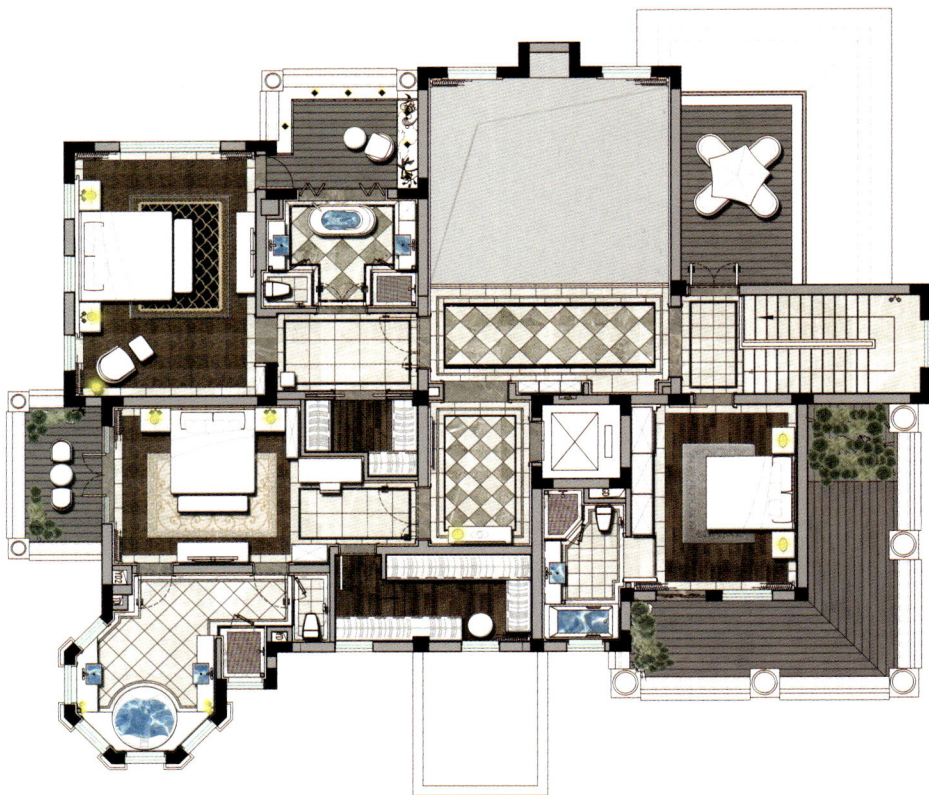

本案设计从简单到繁杂、从整体到局部，镶花刻金，精雕细琢给人一丝不苟的印象。一方面保留了材质、色彩的大致风格，让人感受到传统的历史痕迹与浑厚的文化底蕴，同时又摒弃了过于复杂的肌理和装饰，简化了线条。将怀古的浪漫情怀与现代人对生活的需求相结合，兼容华贵典雅与时尚现代，反映出后工业时代个性化的美学观点和文化品位。

设计师将一楼入口玄关结合电梯厅，形成了由钢琴室、吧台、西餐厅、早餐厅到家庭室组成的一系列串联的生活轨迹。二楼由电梯与楼梯的接入形成双主卧的格局，并加入文化艺廊与客厅挑空的意象。各主卧的浴室各有特色，增加了不少卧室的情趣。

户外庭院由一楼餐厅的烤肉区到地下室的花园形成完整的户外生活的联结。借室内与室外的安排达到相互呼应的最佳效果。地下室与下沉花园充分结合，更突显出书房、台球、SPA、吧台、酒窖等的空间丰富性。

杜柏均

Tu Po Chun

将生活哲学融入个人设计

获得荣誉

2017年 意大利 A'DESIGN AWARD

2017年 中国设计年度人物

2017年 当选"中国室内设计TOP100"榜

2016年 APDC亚太室内设计精英邀请赛

2016年 中国室内设计二十年总评榜——中国室内设计
新锐奖及最具创新设计机构

2016年 金外滩奖

2015年 加拿大GRANDS PRIX DU DESIGN AWARD

2015年 Idea-TOPS艾特国际空间设计奖

让设计回归生活
LET DESIGN RETURN TO LIFE

视界对话杜柏均

杜老师您好，非常感谢您在百忙中抽空接受我们的采访，我深感荣幸。您受邀参加去年上海设计周"再生·当设计遇上可持续"论坛，您主张在设计中融入自己的环保观念，请问您是怎么做到将环保与设计相融合的？

杜柏均： 其实并没有绝对意义上的"环保"，设计师普遍会有很强烈的自我表现欲望，往往不自觉地叠加堆砌，从而衍生出很多不必要的成本。其实设计师只要适当地使用一些手法，比如说材料上可以因地制宜地选择当地特有的材料，就可以很大程度上减少各方面的人力、物力所产生的一系列成本，从而达到相对环保的目的。

除此之外，杜老师您一直强调要将生活哲学融入室内设计，可以跟我们聊聊您的生活哲学吗？与室内设计又有着怎样密不可分的关系？

杜柏均：好像大家听到生活加上"哲学"感觉很神圣，简单来说就是我们的生活态度，日常的生活态度会直接影响到我们的生活。日常生活中一般分为"生理需求"和"心理需求"，好比说喜欢吃美食，有些人会追求色、香、味等，而设计则是在满足生理需求的基础上满足心理需求，而能够满足业主精神追求的设计才能真正地把生存提升为生活。

当下是经济快速发展的时候，社会上也积极倡导环保的消费观念，但有些设计师为了达到奢华效果不惜堆叠大量华贵的软装饰品，杜老师您作为一位环保人士怎么看待这一现象？

杜柏均：我并不排斥华贵的软装饰品，只要它能够带给人赏心悦目的感觉，也不影响及危害他人即可。至于另一种工艺繁复的艺术品或装饰品，我认为摆在合适的位置是对工匠最大的尊重。

台湾的设计有自身显著的特点，您认为台湾室内设计与大陆室内设计有什么不一样的地方？

杜柏均：大陆的设计行业总体来说市场业务量大、甲方的需求比较多元化、空间种类多且包容性强、效率也应市场需求而加快。相对而言台湾市场相对较小、甲方的需求也比较单一化、空间种类也比较匮乏、更注重工艺的把控和细节的雕琢。相比较来说，大陆的设计师在大的市场环境下成长比较迅速，而台湾的设计师基本功相对扎实，会为业主考虑实际使用上的日常习惯。

也就是说大陆要求快节奏、高效率，与台湾的自然、舒适风格形成明显的差异，那么杜老师在您看来是因为地域差异吗？双方有什么利与弊？

杜柏均：大陆因为特定的市场环境使得整体效率偏高，取决于他们的操作方式主要是边设计边执行，从而加速项目进程。而台湾的设计师有更宽裕的工作时间，会通盘考虑整个设计内容达80%~90%以上才会落地执行。市场环境不同就有不一样的应对策略，也没有所谓的利弊。

您作为一位资深设计名师，获得过许多大奖，你认为年轻设计师应该如何看待自己获得的奖项？

杜柏均：我非常鼓励年轻设计师参加各种各样的设计比赛，其目的不单是为了获奖，而是为了能够开拓眼界，在比赛中通过对比学习发现自己的优势与不足，更能激发自己新颖的设计思路。

近些年您有在设计大赛中担任评委，在您看来，一个好的设计项目最看重的应该是什么？做好哪些部分最加分？

杜柏均：一个好的项目最看重整体的协调性，比如整体空间中，平面布置最为重要。至于哪些部分最加分，在我看来，每个部分都很重要。好的项目并不是以所耗费的成本为衡量因素，最好的项目是要符合甲方的要求，在满足设计的同时适当降低成本。这也是设计概论第一课教我们的知识。

室内设计从来不是一个人的工作，杜老师您觉得一个设计团队，应该怎样互相配合才能达到一个完美的工作状态？

杜柏均：设计团队需要有一批有热情、有理想的人，他们充满着热情和憧憬，对设计有自己的目标和理想。每个设计公司都应该去想如何激励团队，让他们自己发掘潜能。团队协作得好可以真正从被动转变为主动。

您是"心+设计学社"的会长，学社里都是国内大咖级别的名师。关于设计，你与其他成员会产生一些不一样的火花吗？

杜柏均：每位老师在各自领域都有自己的"秘籍"，每位社员的交流会互相影响，思想也会互相碰撞，这也是建立"心+设计学社"最主要的目的。受心社成员的影响，我会让团队多练习各个领域的空间而不是只针对项目。团队协作得好可以真正从被动转变为主动。

可以跟我们分享一些在"心+设计学社"比较好玩、印象比较深刻的事情吗？

杜柏均：当然就是米兰三年展，从最初的无人响应到最后的万人响应，整个过程中我们有哭有笑，有血有泪。"一群倔强的老男人，几乎自费500万到米兰参加三年展，7件作品回国之后以151万拍卖捐给偏远地区学校的美术教育。在这么功利与到处花赞助商钱的设计圈里，这12个人是值得大家去鼓励与欣赏的老男人！"

十里洋场拾年华

RECALLING THE YEARS IN OLD SHANGHAI

项目名称 | 汤臣一品

设计公司 | 柏仁设计

设 计 师 | 杜柏均

参与设计 | 王稚云

主要材料 | 墙纸、意大利石材、木里木外墙面系统等

摄 影 师 | 胡文杰

设计理念 | DESIGN CONCEPT

The dream of old Shanghainese started from the side of the Huangpu River. River water comes and goes in vastness freely. Leaning on the window and drawing back the curtains, you'll see architectures rise one after another and tell immortal legends with classic decorative symbols. Nearby, the bell of Customs House rings. Everything is so familiar. This is a unique flavor of this city.

What the owner expects most is a delicate and aristocratic household atmosphere engraved with the classic genre of old Shanghai. So the designer ingeniously reassigns a rational ratio to each space under the original pattern, uses a seemingly simple sliding door to enable the owner to use each space flexibly depending on circumstances and achieves spacious and generous diversified spaces. Using a concise technique, the designer truly restores the emotion and warmth of home to the owner.

Whether in the use of wallpaper or Italian greige stones, the designer tries to interpret the nature of space using a concise technique as far as possible, and finally, he uses bronze lines to sketch the contour of space. The designer hopes to represent the luxury of home delicately using every detail, for example, the faint ink-striped wall. Looking from different angles, you will see the surface glister with different metallic luster. With highlighted maple grains, the functional cabinet and door sheet become more artistic. Coupled with a delicate bronze edging, space soon becomes more brisk and vibrant.

The master bedroom contains the hostess's double locker room, rest room, living room and sleep area. The designer builds this space completely in accordance with the standard of tailoring to make it comfortable and prominent.

卫生间

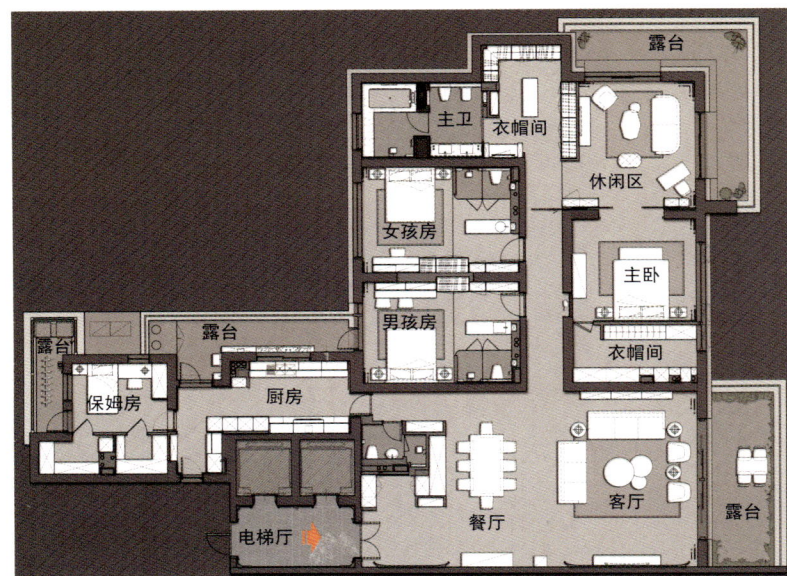

　　老上海人的梦是从黄浦江畔开始的，江水带着自由的心茫茫地来，又茫茫地去。倚在窗前，拉开窗幔，建筑此起彼伏，带着经典的装饰符号诉说着不朽的传说。不远处海关大楼传来的钟声回响，这一切是那么的熟悉，那是这座城所独有的气息。

　　印刻着老上海的经典，精致而不失贵族气息的家居氛围是业主最期望的。因此设计师巧妙地在原有格局下重新分配了每个空间的合理使用比例，并用看似简单的移门闭合让各区域可以依情况弹性使用，实现宽敞大方的多元空间，以简练的手法把家的情感与温暖真正还原到业主的手中。

　　无论是运用墙纸还是意大利米灰色石材，都尽可能采用简练的设计手法来诠释空间本质的美，最后用上古铜的金属线条勾勒出空间的精神。设计师希望那份家的奢华是通过对每一个细节精心地处理去展现，例如隐约的墨纹墙面，在不同的角度望去，面上会呈现不同的金属光泽，配上高光质感的枫影木纹，使得功能性的柜体及门片变得更具艺术性，加上细致的古铜收边，让空间瞬间灵动更有生命力。

　　主卧室里包含了女主人的更衣室、卫生空间、起居室和睡眠区域，设计师完全按私人订制的标准来打造这个空间，舒适而显赫。

The room of two kids is carefully designed with an open restroom. Without losing functionality and convenience, space is freed. Each area is concise and orderly. Only such a space with fine craftsmanship can truly bring out the owner's attention to the quality of life.

Look at both sides of the Huangpu River. Recall the past of the river. The scene is spectacular. This is the resplendence of Oriental Paris, and also the charm of the home.

两个孩子的房间，精心策划了半开放性的卫生空间，在保留功能与便利性的同时将空间解放出来，每个区域简练有序，而这精致工艺烘托的空间，才能真正衬托出业主对生活品质的追求。

看浦江两岸，忆海上往昔，那景象是壮观的，这是东方巴黎的璀璨，也是家的魅力。

探究设计哲学，量身订制居所

EXPLORING THE PHILOSOPHY OF DESIGN,
DESIGNING THE TAILORED RESIDENCE

视界对话王俊宏

森境室内装修设计工程有限公司
王俊宏建筑设计咨询(上海)有限公司
创始人、设计总监

王俊宏

Luke Wang

汉学美感哲思所引导，我们将"形"的
哲学，实践于空间的美感中

获得荣誉

2017年 漂亮家居新秀设计师奖

2016年 DULUX COLOUR AWARD

2015年13th MODERN DECORATION INTERNATIONAL
MEDIA AWARD

2015年 JINTANG PRIZE年度优秀办公空间设计

2014年 TID AWARD居住空间类

2014年 百大人气设计师人气奖

2014年 JINTANG PRIZE年度优秀住宅公寓设计

2014年 中国厨房设计奖

2014年 22th APIDA DESIGN AWARD住宅类等

王老师您好！我看到贵公司的官网上讲"汉学美感哲思所引导"，其中的"汉学美感"具体指什么？在室内装修设计中，您是如何呈现这些美感的呢？

王俊宏：所谓汉学美感，其实是东方文化的代表。当今室内设计深受20世纪初的建筑大师柯布西耶 (Le Corbusier) 现代主义思维的影响，但我们也不该轻易舍弃中国几千年文化所积累的设计美学，因此我在设计上，希望将东、西文化融合，使得"中学为体，西学为用"。即使用利落的现代线条来表现，也希望透过色彩、图腾的暗喻，让设计"接地气"，展现不同的文化特质，而非全盘复制西方设计。

您把空间设计比喻为"参加一场一生一次的难得盛宴"，这背后有什么原因或故事吗？

王俊宏：对每位委托设计的业主来说，或许穷尽毕生之力，才能购置一套房，因此设计者必然要戮力以赴，把每一次的设计，当成一生一次的难得盛宴，恭谨、细心、面面俱到，才不辜负业主的信任与期待。这一场盛宴，设计者、业主、施工者都参与其中，缺一不可。一场宴席的圆满，非一己之力能够独撑，而是靠大家一起努力，才能成就空间的美好。

近几年，您在设计中加入了很多花艺设计，公司的软装装饰部更有植艺风格师。对于花艺设计，您觉得最大的特点和心得是什么？

王俊宏：初出茅庐的时候，做设计总是以满足自己对空间美感的苛求为依据。随着年龄渐长，接触的业主愈来愈多，渐渐体会到，空间其实是用来生活的，于是开始留意所有生活细节，将很多软装物件纳入设计计划中，花艺设计就是其中之一。例如以前总是依标准规格或业主的身高来配置桌椅、台面高度，当花艺纳入设计计划中，就得依照赏玩角度，做出微幅调整，因此，每一个物件的安排，不仅必须符合人体工学，也得关照视觉的整体美，使得设计考量不再单一化，反而变得复杂而有微妙差异。这微妙的差异，往往让人有"失之毫厘，差之千里"的感受，这就是我们现在所追求的"高端量身订制"概念。

贵公司的作品追求"随物赋形"，于细微处构筑美好，文案充满文化气息，侃侃而谈，那么您怎么看待作品本身与文案之间的关系呢？

王俊宏：若把苏轼的"随物赋形"翻译成现代设计语言，那就是西方提倡的"形随机能"。我们在空间设计中采用的所有造型，并非单纯为造型而生，而是密切结合生活机能，"实用"是必要条件，而造型则会随着机能变化。通过设计者的巧手慧心而改变，设计的专业与力道，也将从中窥见端倪，分出高下。当我们的文案歌咏着空间造型之美，其实很多设计细节也就隐藏在可见的造型之中，只是没有说破。我们用造型之美将实用机能美化，但所有设计的滥觞其实是从生活机能而来。

在《城市绘》中，您为什么会想到请艺术家Joseph Chen以屋主一家四口的人像为主题创作彩绘，以及定制一家人的肖像画抱枕？通过二者表现出来的广受好评的"丑"，您想传达一些什么？

王俊宏：邀请艺术家Joseph Chen为《城市绘》绘制壁画，其实是希望能在空间中表现幽默感与设计的趣味。因为Joseph Chen的画风向来以凸显人物特征为主，而非完美、工笔、写实。之所以用这样的方式来表现，其实与居住者具有年轻、活泼的心与开放的态度有关，若屋主较严肃、一丝不苟，不可能接受这样的设计提案，也就无法成就《城市绘》这样的空间作品。

我们知道您先是在台湾发展，之后在上海等地创办公司，想必您对台湾和大陆的设计都有比较深刻的见解，能和我们说说吗？对于二者的异同，您是如何借鉴的呢？

王俊宏："入境问俗"不仅是对旅人的提醒，也是对在台湾、上海、深圳皆设点的我的提醒，是做设计时必须谨守的分寸。即使同文同种，各地依然存在显著文化差异，因此做设计时，势必得拿掉惯性，深入了解不同文化，才能做到心坎里。其实设计原本就是因人而异的，每个人身家背景不同，也会有不同的好恶。就好比酿制红酒，即使葡萄品种相同，用不同风土条件下生长的葡萄酿出来的酒，也会有极大的差异。不论身处台湾、北京、上海、深圳、香港，做设计时，我们务求"高端量身订制"，让每个案子因环境、文化、个人特质而有截然不同的表现，符合每位委托者的要求与期待。

跨越海峡两岸的两家公司都需要您投入精力，您是怎样平衡公司管理与设计工作的？

王俊宏：我其实还没什么资格侃侃而谈管理的艺术，毕竟公司是逐步发展成现在的规模，我自己也处于边做边学的状态，亲力亲为是必然，因为很多事不能假手他人。但当规模逐渐变大，就得培养优秀的团队，而自己则变成整合团队的领头羊，负责定下公司的大方向，通过分工合作的方式，让大家朝相同目标前进，就好比划船，若各自为政，就会原地打转，一旦群策群力，就能快速达阵。

工作中的您和生活中的您差别大吗？工作之余您喜欢做些什么？

王俊宏：工作与生活其实有截然不同的步调，工作必然是快节奏，有很多必须决断的事项，丝毫不能犹豫。虽然不能悠闲过日子，但我学会了在忙碌的工作中如何忙里偷闲，或许用半小时的空档，沏一壶好茶，仔细拿捏泡茶的时间、使用的茶叶量，找出今年春茶，该怎么泡最好喝。品茗的当下，所有思绪都集中于此，烦心事暂且抛开，彻底放空、放慢脚步，才能懂得好茶的滋味与生活的原味。

您对于将来的公司和人生有什么样的定位和规划？

王俊宏：人生其实往往是"计划赶不上变化"，我觉得只要做好分内的事，磨练自己的专业技能，让自己与公司都处于最佳状态，就是最好的计划，因为只要蓄势待发，机会就会降临在准备好的人身上，一切都水到渠成。

"旅行是一个丰富自己的最好方式，阅读也是一种短暂的逃难，像穿越时空般，拿起一本历史文学文籍，马上就掉入了那样一个年代情景里，得以暂时抽离。"您常常在旅行和阅读中寻找灵感，通过对生活细心的观察去找到解决空间难题的办法。在旅行和阅读中，您有遇到特别有意思的至今仍记忆犹新的事情吗？

王俊宏：前段时间和太太带着两个孩子到云南旅行，旅程很艰难，但孩子们的表现却超越大人对他们的刻板印象。本以为他们吃不了苦，但他们的毅力与体力却超乎我们的期待，爬山的时候，甚至远远将我们抛在后面。这件事让我深刻体会到，孩子是父母最好的学习榜样，当了父母，就能在孩子们身上，重新学习，找到存在的意义，获得力量。

低调隐市 用画绘家

A LOW-KEY HOME DECORATED BY PAINTING

项目名称 | 城市绘

设计公司 | 森境室内装修设计工程有限公司

设 计 师 | 王俊宏、蓝介泽、陈新治

项目地点 | 台湾台北

项目面积 | 160 ㎡

主要材料 | 钢刷木皮、黑板漆、烤漆、雾面石英砖、木百也门等

摄 影 师 | KPS黄钰崴

艺 术 家 | Joseph Chen

设计理念 | DESIGN CONCEPT

Space is originally an old house in the center of the city. The complex beam column structure compresses the distance between the sky and ground, forming a sense of oppression, and the compartment which does not meet the requirements obscures the lighting and ventilation. Through the attitude of breakthrough and creativity, the designer opened the pattern, introduced adequate natural lights for indoor, and used the artificial lighting in the insufficient areas. The long public area has the best light, and the designer left the dining area and kitchen for condensing the family's feelings and made the hostess who loves cooking can interact with her family at any time.

There is an axis extended from island bar to dining table, which is the continuation of the comfortable sofa area of living room. The blackboard painting behind the sofa was painted by a famous painter. The family images which are painted on the spot are in a unique cartoon style, while the pillows in the same style also make people smile. The bedroom continues the same low-key and restrained style, and the thoughtful pattern arrangement allocating with the design of composite functional desk highlights the precious of costful urban residence. Surrounded by the low-key gray color, this space shows a warm and happy home.

Although this space is only a part of this city, it is the axis of family. In the morning light and evening mist, this space is filled with warm and abundant emotion. The beauty of design is not complicated and gorgeous, but neat and plain like ukiyo-e using the concise lines to outline the daily life of ordinary people and telling the eternal value of a home with the feasible design.

空间原本是位于市中心的旧宅，复杂的梁柱结构压缩纵向距离，形成压迫感，不符需求的隔间遮蔽了采光和通风。设计师以大破大立的态度，将格局打开，为室内引进充足的自然光，并在仍不足之处以人工照明辅助。长形的公共区拥有最佳光线，设计师留给凝聚家人情感的餐、厨区，让热爱烹饪的女主人随时能与家人互动。

中岛吧台至餐桌轴线一路延伸，接续的是舒适宜人的客厅沙发区。沙发后的黑板墙画作出自名家之手，现场绘制的家人形象带着特立独行的漫画风，而出于同门的抱枕也让人会心一笑。卧室延续相同的低调与内敛风格，贴心的格局安排，搭配复合机能的书桌设计，彰显出都市住宅寸土寸金的珍贵。在灰阶低调的色彩环绕下，空间酝酿着属于家的温暖和幸福。

空间虽只是城市拼图的一隅，却是家人生活的轴心，于晨曦微光中、暮霭柔光下，满溢着温暖、丰沛的情感。而设计的美好亦不在于繁复与华丽，而在于利落与平实，如同浮世绘般以简洁的线条，勾勒市井小民的日常，用不浮夸的设计述说一个家永恒的价值。

唐忠汉

近境制作 设计总监

TT

以最真诚的人文精神，诉说着
空间的故事

获得荣誉

2017年 荣获德国红点传达设计奖 Red dot communication award

2017年 荣获日本优良设计奖 Good design Award

2017年 荣获英国国际地产大奖亚太区 Asia Pacific Property Awards

2017年 荣获香港亚洲建+设大奖 A&D Trophy Awards

2017年 荣获台湾室内设计大奖 Taiwan Interior design award

2017年 荣获意大利 A' Design Award & Competition

2017年 荣获居然杯CIDA 中国室内设计大奖

2017年 荣获中国北斗名师最佳物质领域设计奖

2016年 荣获意大利 A' Design Award & Competition

2016年 荣获韩国设计大奖 K–Design Award

2016年 荣获美国国际设计奖 international design award

2015年 荣获英国室内设计节 INSIDE World Festival of Interiors 住宅空间大奖等

追求本真，不忘初心
PURSUING THE GENUINENESS, KEEPING
THE ORIGINAL MIND

视界对话唐忠汉

唐老师好，首先感谢您这么多年来对视界出版的支持，您的设计也是越来越有味道，可以跟我们
聊聊您这些年在设计上最大的变化是什么？

唐忠汉：这些年在做设计的时候，一开始是在追求自己心中想象的画面，在这个过程中我们接触
了不同的人群、市场、更多的机会往全国各地开始做设计。由于所看的、所接触的更广阔，给了
我们更多的契机和想象，而在设计的过程中我们希望能够保持自己原本的纯粹，能把各区域当地

所独有的生活方式和生活个性表现出来。所以这些年我们在不断适应、变化和调整，以达到市场需求和自己想象之间的平衡。接受不一样的挑战，在气候上、风土人情上都会有许多不一样的思考，是这两年在设计中比较明显的不同。

哪些设计理念是您一直坚持的？

唐忠汉： 在设计过程中从建筑出发的设计理念，对所有物件、物质的思考，包含到所有空间的条件、它的构成方式、组成方式等从建筑元素出发，是我们在设计中非常重要的环节。而更多回归到人的部分，我们开始探讨需求，即机能跟造型之间的联系，机能让真实的需求被照顾到，透过设计者的用心，以更贴心的方式做一些前所未有的突破。因此，细心地照顾每一个环节，掌握好尺寸，对所有行为的可能性以及任何一种材料的适用和耐用的不同程度分析，关注心理强度部分。从室内建筑、到形式机能、到内心强度这几件事情，都是我们设计理念一直坚持和强调的。

您一直强调建筑与室内的延续性，也特别擅长自然原始风、简约机能风，做好这些风格，有什么诀窍吗？最需要注意的是什么？

唐忠汉： 如果透过建筑上面的思考，去考虑室内构成的一些元素，自然就会由外而内、或者由内而外的移动和延续。强调自然跟简约机能，是为了把人的元素，人的因素不断凸显出来。把握人与所需要的自然元素：音、光、热、气、水之间的关联性，才能给人提供真正需要宜居的生活。它不需要披金戴银，掌握好的空气、好的温度、好的生活品质这些自然的元素，才更贴近人本主义，回归以人为本的建筑思考，从人的角度探讨他的需求以后，将表象的需求元素反映到内心世界的哲学层面去思考，更能体现出居住者对空间的期待。所以，我们运用很多自然的材质，通过建筑的手法，去强调以人为本的建筑设计，把机能、造型等，空间整体化，最终回归到对人的观察，对人的重视，强调人本、人文的空间概念。

您一直强调自然元素，在您的作品中，我们也都可以明显感受到材质的肌理、光影的律动，仿佛作品本身就会表达，这就是您一直追求的设计表达吗？

唐忠汉： 是的是的。我们希望能够透过材质、光线这些本身所有建筑的室内设计手法，去表达我们的作品，能通过这些触动居住者内心一些哲学层面的思考，对物质、对材质、对人的感觉。所以，在空间中你看到的不仅仅是某一种材料，带给居住者的可能是一种时间感，是一种温暖，是一种不同的情绪反应。而这些材质、肌理的表现在光影律动中是最重要的一个部分，透过材料本身，表达出某种特定的情绪记忆，光线加入，把我们的造型更加凸显出来，而过滤、处理过的光线，让光影跟空间想象形成更好的连结。

近期您有很多项目都在大陆，如跟朱周设计一起合作的北京金茂府，未来您会继续扩大大陆市场吗？有没有一些特别想要合作的设计公司？

唐忠汉： 这一两年正好有机会接触到不同的专案，很多都在大陆市场，我自己本身也希望能够持续与更多优秀的设计公司进行碰撞，有更多的机会接触到不同领域、不同层面的设计公司。像国内很多顶级的设计公司，我都会非常希望将来有接触到的可能。我们最近在做的一些案子，同一个项目里，会遇见吴滨老师的案场、梁建国老师的案场等，都能让我们从旁得到更多的学习机会，对于这样的机会，我们非常珍惜。

唐忠汉

TT

以最真诚的人文精神，诉说
着空间的故事

对于合作公司的选择，您会从哪些方面来衡量是否作为合作对象？

唐忠汉： 首先在理念上面的一致是非常重要的，我们认为的美，我们认为的空间，我们认为所要表达的最终形态，是不是一致，只有这样才有机会做出一个共同的作品。所以在设计理念上面的看法，尊重的部分是合作上面非常重要的一个参考环节。

您本身作为国际大奖上的常客，对于获奖有什么心得感触吗？

唐忠汉： 做设计的过程其实是一个非常辛苦、非常孤独的奋斗过程。我们希望在这个路途中所追求的不单单只是业绩、或者完成项目的委托，我们更多的希望是把它当做一个有情感的作品，把我们对新事物的期待，透过它能够反射出来。在做这件事情的时候，能够忘掉那些孤独，锁定心里面的目标，把作品呈现出来，让别人可以切实感受到你想要表达作品的一些想法和情感。所以，获奖其实是让观众解读出我们作品所要表达的情绪、情感和故事。

此外，在很多设计盛典上您都会以嘉宾或评委的身份出现，对于年轻设计师，多参加评选有好处吗？应该以什么样的心态去面对获奖？

唐忠汉： 在设计过程中以参赛目的去竞争，其实是一个让我们重新检视自己的机会和方法。一路上狂奔、前进，项目一个接一个，事情没有终止的一天。获奖其实是一个很好的结点，提醒自己回头看看曾经做过的东西，思索一些理念，回溯审视自己，把之前没有想透的东西重新来认真思考。如果以自我整理的心态去面对获奖这件事情，在整个过程中，你会有不一样的感受和体会。所以，我会建议年轻的设计师多多参加，这样可以带给你更多的机会重新检视自己，整理自己，把这一路上的累积，转化成对自己设计路上的鼓励，同时也可以通过这样的学习对未来设计有新的感悟。

因为近几年掀起了新东方、新中式风格的浪潮，作为独立的设计师该不该跟风？确立自己的设计风格是不是有必要的？为什么？

唐忠汉： 追求任何风格的浪潮都是一个短暂的行为，事情都会过去。你可以试着回想一年前的一些事情，你会发现你已经记不起来，很多记忆会随着时间而淡化、离开。作为一个独立设计师，不应该跟风，而应该确立自己独立的设计风格是首要的，必须努力的。人做的很多努力都是为了要寻找自己、遇见自己、找到自己。其实一开始做设计不一定要做某一种风格，只是把自己想要表达的呈现出来，然后单纯地不断去尝试，再更加了解自己。有段话很有意思，是这样的："'自己'这个东西是看不见的，撞上一些别的什么，反弹回来，才会了解'自己'。所以，跟很强的东西、可怕的东西、水准很高的东西相碰撞，然后，才知道'自己'是什么，这才是自我。"这就是遇见挫折之后的正面思考，更能了解自己。而设计师确立自己风格，等同于认识自己，清楚自己的想要，明确自己的追求，是一辈子应该坚持的事情。

最后，可以谈谈未来国内室内设计的发展吗？或者对未来一代年轻设计师有什么期许呢？

唐忠汉： 现在国内室内设计环境蓬勃发展，达到前所未有、难以想象的境界。我们现在走出国际，被国际上的友人礼遇、尊重、给予很高的肯定和评价，就像我们刚刚所提到的东方风格，它不仅仅是在一个区域，甚至全球，都会有一个脉络和潮流，这是在众多中国设计者的努力发展之下形成的一个非常好的状态。

对于国内设计发展的过程当中我希望能更多的从自我着手，找到真正需要的、累积的，而不是看外面已经做好、做成的，这需要我们在自己发展的过程中，越来越清楚地知道自己的调性，坚持自己的方式。在蓬勃发展的大环境中，通过大家的努力让设计产业有更高的视野。

而对于未来年轻一代设计师希望回归到态度上，学习怎么样以好的态度去设计，养成良好的人格，找寻到真正面对设计的态度，而非单纯地追求利益，凸显自己，找到真正的设计魅力。在面对要求和挑战的时候，以更积极、更热血、更正面的态度去面对，这样我们才能有更好的环境，维护我们的文化。最后回归人本层面，希望我们能遇见最好的自己，变成更好的自己。

空间对话 人文居所

SPACE DIALOGUE, CULTURAL RESIDENCE

项目名称 I 北京金茂府

设计公司 I 近境制作

设 计 师 I 唐忠汉、卜筠真

项目地点 I 北京

项目面积 I 190 ㎡

主要材料 I 石材、实木皮、木地板、镀钛、
喷漆、绷布、壁纸等

摄 影 师 I VMA VISUAL

设计理念 | DESIGN CONCEPT

The central axis in Beijing refers to the central axis of Beijing city in Yuan, Ming, and Qing Dynasties. The urban planning of Beijing is characterized by the bilateral symmetry centering on the Forbidden City north to the Bell and Drum Tower, south to the Yongding Gate through the north and south of Beijing. This is the longest central axis of the city in the world, having a highly praise as the "backbone of the city" of Beijing. Liang Sicheng, the famous Chinese architect, had said, "The unique, sublime order of Beijing was formed by the establishment of this central axis." More importantly, it is always full of growing vitality. For more than 700 years, it closely related to every historic change of the city.

While the central axis is extending, and Beijing is expanding. Half a century ago, Jane Jacobs had questioned, "The city we built

is exactly for cars or people?" In fact, no matter how the central axis changes, the ultimate goal of the city is to provide a better life and a more appropriate development opportunity for people. Nowadays, the progress and busyness of times not only sacrifice the "quality" of living but also cause great pressure to city traffic and the communication among people. From the thinking space of human nature, we can achieve the goal of ideal life.

The real meaning of home is not the composition of members, but the most important thing is the exchange of emotion and life. In the design concept, the designer not only thinks about life as a resident, but also needs to use the "essence of life" as a starting point to connect a new life experience.

In every field, the designer abandons the understanding of the usage of original space in living space. While we can divide the space into the public area for the concept of emotional communication and the quiet and independent private area. The public area is divided by the vertical axis which the south begins with the constitution of the square hall, living room, dining room and social kitchen. In the whole space, for keeping the landscape as far as possible from a wide perspective, we get rid of unnecessary colors and modelings, and reduce the cramped feeling of the vision. The four spaces delineate the ambiguous four-dimensional space to make life not just passing by, but will stack with each other. At the end of the hall is a completely free and eased corner; the living room is a space for social communication; the dining room is a space for decent dining and having a dialogue with family; while the design of the social kitchen is an important and special space which is the most common connection of life contact and emotional communication.

In addition, the study, master bedroom and master bathroom are planned in the South horizontal axis. The open setting of study is regarded as the extension of the master bedroom's functions and the multi-functional usage space. The bedrooms on the central axis of north give appropriate independent privacy for the different living habits among different generations. But through the guidance of moving line, it can adjust the distance and temperature between each other in time to make everyone living in it find a comfortable living form with family. These four public spaces constitute the public area with a common character that is "dialogue". This is the thinking space for this case.

　　北京中轴线是指元、明、清时的北京城的中轴线，北京的城市规划具有以宫城为中心左右对称的特点，北起钟鼓楼，南至永定门，贯穿京城南北。这条世界上现存最长的城市中轴线，盛赞为北京的"城市脊梁"。中国著名建筑大师梁思成曾说过"北京独有的壮美秩序就由这条中轴线的建立而产生"。更重要的是，它始终充满生长的活力。700多年来，城市的每一次历史性变局，都与之息息相关。

　　然而中轴线在延伸，北京城在扩张。"我们建设城市，究竟是为汽车，还是为人？"半个世纪前，Jane Jacobs 这样质问。其实，无论中轴线如何变化，城市最终的目的是为了给人们提供更好的生活、更适宜的发展机会。现在时代的进步与忙碌牺牲了人居的"质"，也给城市交通还有人与人的交流造成了极大压力。而从人性上的思索空间，更可以达到理想生活的目标。

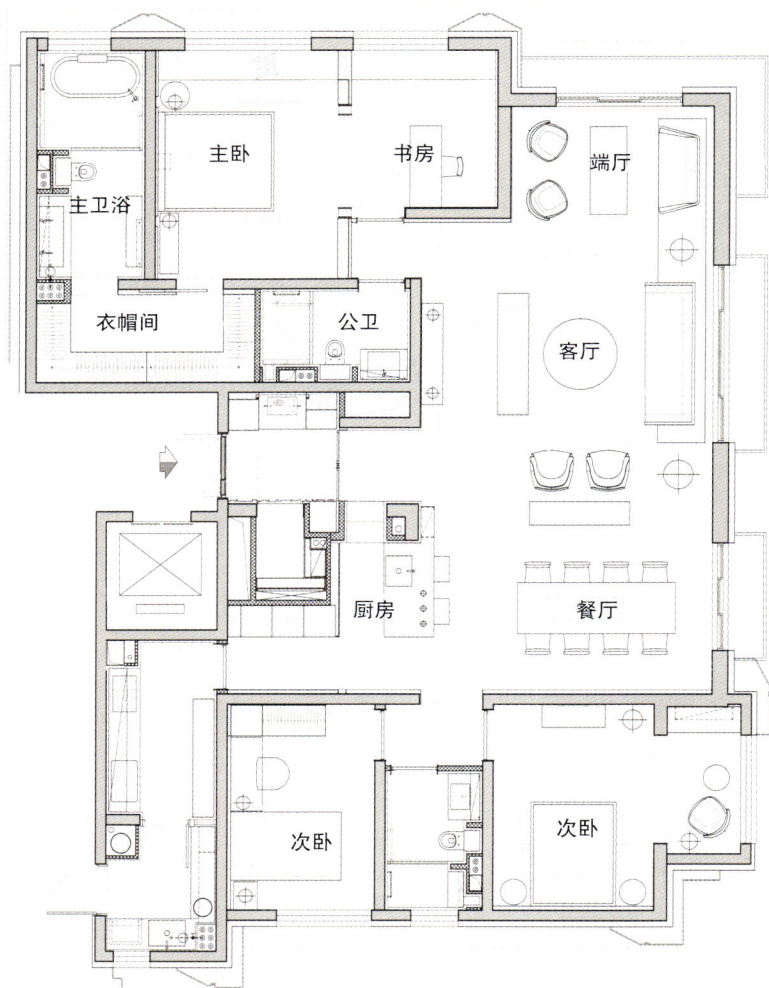

家真正的意义，不只是成员上的组成，最重要的是感情与生活上的交流。设计想法中除了要感同身受的以居住者去思考生活，也需要"从生活本质"为出发，串联出新的生活体验。

在各个场域舍弃了一般人在居住空间上既有的空间使用上的认知。而我们在空间的赋予上，概分为感情交流概念的公共区域，以及静谧独立的私密空间。公共空间经由垂直轴线的划分，南向开始以端厅、客厅、餐厅、社交厨房所组成，而在整体空间尽可能保留景观面的广阔视角下，我们摒除多余的色彩跟造型，减少了视觉上的局促感，四个空间勾划出模糊暧昧的四维空间，使得生活不只是擦肩而过，而是会互相堆栈。端厅是悠游自在的角落，客厅是交际畅谈的空间，餐厅是端庄用餐与家庭对话的场所，而社交厨房此设计内为重要的特殊空间，是生活接触上与感情交流上最为平凡的串联。

此外将书房、主卧、主卫浴三个空间规划在南位水平轴线上，书房开放式的设定，视为主卧机能上的延伸，也是多功能使用空间。北位水平轴线上的卧室，对于不同世代之间的起居习惯，给予适当的独立私密性，但通过动线的带领，却也适时的调整彼此之间的距离与温度，让生活在其中的每个人找到与家人相处的舒服形态。四个空间组成的公共空间，有个共通性质，即是"对话"，这就是此案例想做出的思考空间。

Each district is connected and communicated with each other through an open vision, and creates a corner of living space suitable for the whole age. In the usage of materials, the public space uses the light color stone as the allocation with the main color which is the moist wood veneer, and takes advantages of iron pieces to describe the personality of the material without any unnecessary decorations. It only presents the original texture and color of the stone, highlights the warm feeling of wood, and makes people trapped in this environment be away from the hustle and bustle of the city without any burden. The private area uses the cloth with a soft rhyme to create a relaxed and secluded space. In this comfortable space, one can enjoy the "abandoning" and "be restarting". Moreover, it also considers the aging lifestyle and integrates the elements of health and technology in addition to the use of spatial scales. Whether it is the emotional connection in the social kitchen, or the integration of health and technology, forms the combination and superposition of function and emotion with the living concept of "city ideal of one square kilometer" proposed by this case, which is starting from the needs of "human". The living space or architectural ideas are based on this as the significance of thinking.

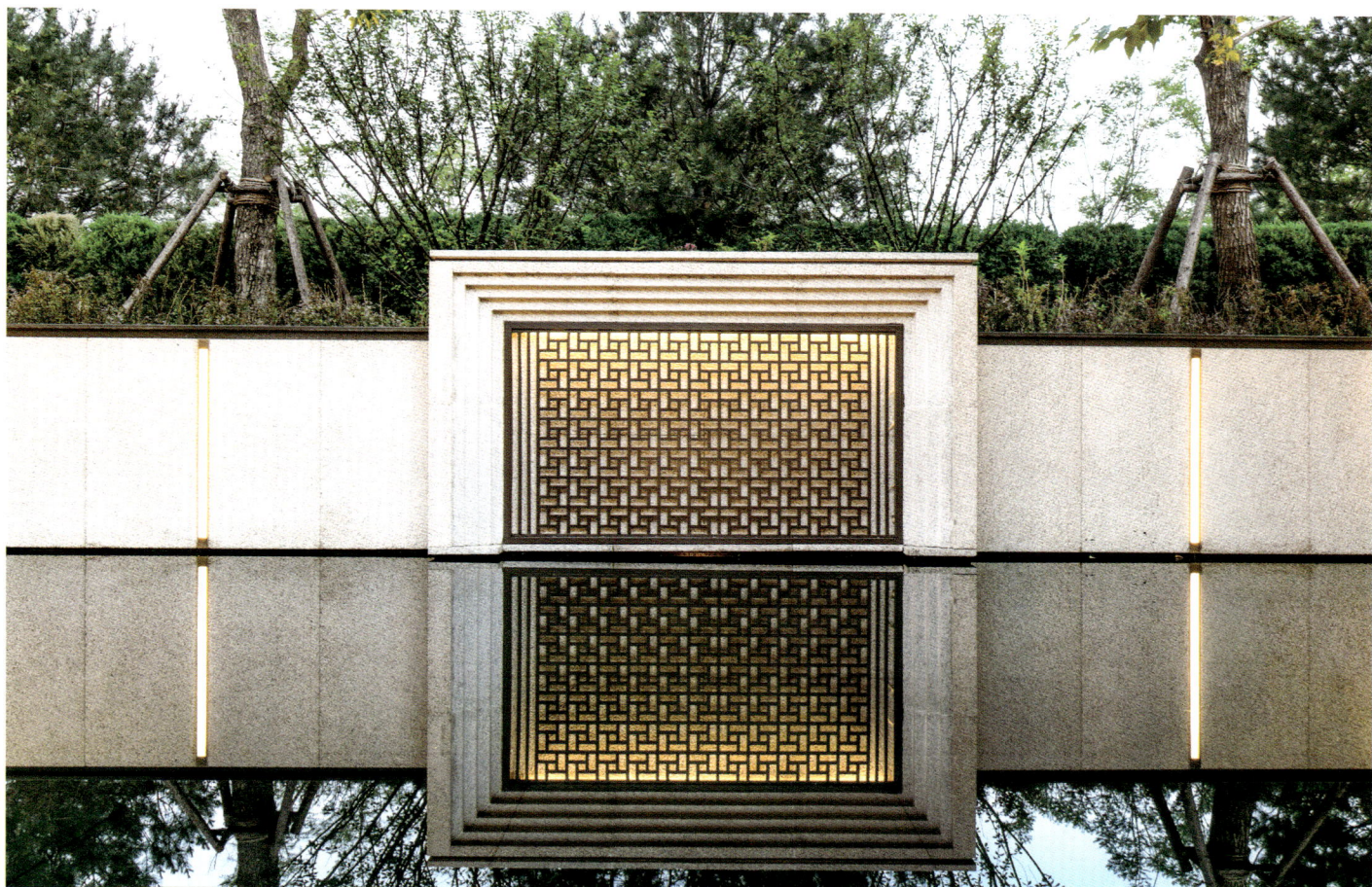

  各区通过开放的视野互相联系与交流，制造出全年龄段生活空间的角落。材料的运用上公共空间使用偏浅色系的石材与温润的木皮做为主色调的搭配，再利用铁件去刻划材料的个性，不做过多的装饰，只呈现石材原始的纹理与色泽，也将木质感受的温暖跳脱出来，让深陷此境的人可以无负担地远离白天的喧嚣。私密空间则是使用柔韵的布料营造出放松隐逸的空间，在这舒适的场域享受的是"放下"与"重新开始"。再者，也考虑到适老化的生活型态，除了在空间尺度上的运用，也将健康与科技的元素整合在一起。无论是社交厨房上的感情串联，或是健康与科技的整合，与此案所提出"一平方公里的城市理想"的生活概念，从"人"的需求为出发，进而形成功能与情感上的复合与加叠。居住空间或是建筑理念皆以此基础为思考的意义。

赵睿

Zhao Rui

纬图建筑设计装饰工程有限公司
董事长、设计总监

汲取自然养分，构筑理想的生活形态

获得荣誉

荣获香港APIDA亚太区设计大奖 金奖&银奖

荣获意大利A'DESIGN AWARD 金奖&铜奖

荣获法国IF DESIGN AWARD

荣获加拿大GRANDS PRIX DU DESIGN–SPECIAL AWARD

荣获KAPOK红棉中国设计奖 室内设计至尊奖

荣获台湾GOLDEN PIN DESIGN AWARD金点设计奖

荣获IAI DESIGN AWARD 最佳设计大奖

荣获CIID中国室内设计大奖 金奖1&银奖2&铜奖2

荣获CIID中国室内设计大奖 最佳设计企业2

荣获APDC亚太室内设计精英邀请赛 金奖

荣获现代装饰国际传媒奖 年度餐饮空间大奖

荣获I–DING AWARD艾鼎奖 餐饮空间金奖

荣获筑巢奖–餐饮空间金奖

荣获JINTANG PRIZE金堂奖 年度十佳餐饮空间设计

荣获IDG金创意奖 金奖&银奖

不断追寻设计的新源泉

PERSUING THE SOURCE OF DESIGN
CONTINUALLY

视界对话赵睿

赵老师好，非常荣幸采访到您，一直被您设计里强烈的自然人文气息吸引，《葫芦岛食屋餐厅》《管宅》都是。在设计中，您是比较偏爱自然元素吗？

赵睿：也许是吧，我也不太确定，因为每个项目的性质都不太一样，只是这两个项目位置都刚好处于海边，有很好的自然环境，我就选择了与自然融合的方法去表现。

您既是建筑师又是室内设计师，要同时把建筑与室内，您觉得在做设计时哪些点是特别需要注意的？

赵睿： 每个项目除了对建筑及室内情况的了解，还要结合客户对空间设计的期望及要求，表达风格的同时还需要从材料、家具及艺术品的选择多方融入去诠释空间想表达的意境。

在设计《管宅》时，是带着怎样的出发点？

赵睿： 让业主更好的感受自然，给他一个更好的生活环境。

这是一个改建和加建的项目，项目的时间跨度比较长，在完成过程中我常常涌现出许多新的想法，状态不停发生变化，在不同的阶段都会加入新的想法进去，可以说这是各种想法"堆砌"出来的一个作品。

《管宅》因此也收获了很多奖项的肯定，对此您有什么感受？

赵睿： 当然是非常高兴，哈哈（笑），往下需要更坚持和更努力工作。

纬图官网首页写着"我们+一起+建筑+生活"，您也一直强调设计是一种习惯，可以跟我们具体聊聊您的设计理念吗？

赵睿： 我的理念就是在不停地寻找，因为没有终点，寻找各种各样的感受，这就是我的生活，这不一定完全是设计方面，对于我来说设计和生活是很难分清楚的。

生活中您是怎样的生活状态？跟您的设计风格一样吗？

赵睿： 也许是吧，生活中的我是一时一个样，

我的思维会受到不同事物的影响，不断产生新的想法，各种想法我都希望能去尝试，这让我有一种兴奋感。

可以谈谈您理想中的设计生活吗？

赵睿： 我只能说，一直以来我还是相对满意我的设计生活的，我只能让自己这样想，如果欲望没有边际，是会很痛苦的。

比如我对很多生活方式都很向往，都想去参与，但我只有在工作的状态下才是安静和专一的。说回来，原本我的工作和生活也是分不开的，那对于我来说就是理想的设计生活了。

另外，我们在您的作品文件中可以欣赏到很多漂亮的手绘图，也有一些设计草稿图，而现在很多设计师基本采用效果图，您平时做设计都会先做手绘图吗？

赵睿： 偶尔吧，20多年前我是专门做手绘效果图工作的，所以现在偶尔也会画一下草图，把手绘当作多会使用一种工具，也算多一个兴趣爱好。

您作为国内设计风格比较鲜明的设计名师，对于未来设计有什么期待或者规划吗？

赵睿： 我是尽量过好每一天，享受每刻过程，尽力做好一些事情的人。

对我来说是没有计划的，一切都是顺其自然。大大小小的计划可能都是为了完成你要做的任务或项目，过程中自然而然会遇到很多问题，只能见招拆招，一个一个去处理。我希望能做出更多更好的作品，我所做的一切都围绕这个目标，可以说有计划，也可以说没计划。

CREATING A MANSION WITH BEST SCENERY CAREFULLY

精雕细刻

打造顶级风景豪宅

项目名称 | 管宅

设计公司 | 纬图设计有限公司

设 计 师 | 赵睿

参与设计 | 李龙君、刘方圆、叶增辉等

艺术创作 | 朝鲁门、伍启雕

项目地点 | 海南三亚

项目面积 | 7300 ㎡

主要材料 | 山东白锈石、俄罗斯松木、质感漆等

摄 影 师 | 张骑麟

设计理念 | DESIGN CONCEPT

In this project, we hope everywhere is full of the scenery, picture, light, mood and practical details of life, so we are greedy to show all the requirements in the design.

The project is located in Haitang Bay, Sanya. It is a holiday residence and small private club hotel. There are 12 rooms, including dining area, public area and entertainment area. When the project was first received, it was an unfinished building, so our main task is to carry out its construction and structural transformation, to complete the project from indoor to outdoor in details, and to deliver the project.

The local climate of Sanya is hot with scorching sun. The building is located in the seaside so that the sea breeze is particularly hard, and the seawater has high salinity and strong corrosiveness. Thus, the choice of materials is very important for the quality of the whole project. Finally, the designer selected white rust stone from Shandong, log, and texture paint these three kinds of high durability decorative materials.

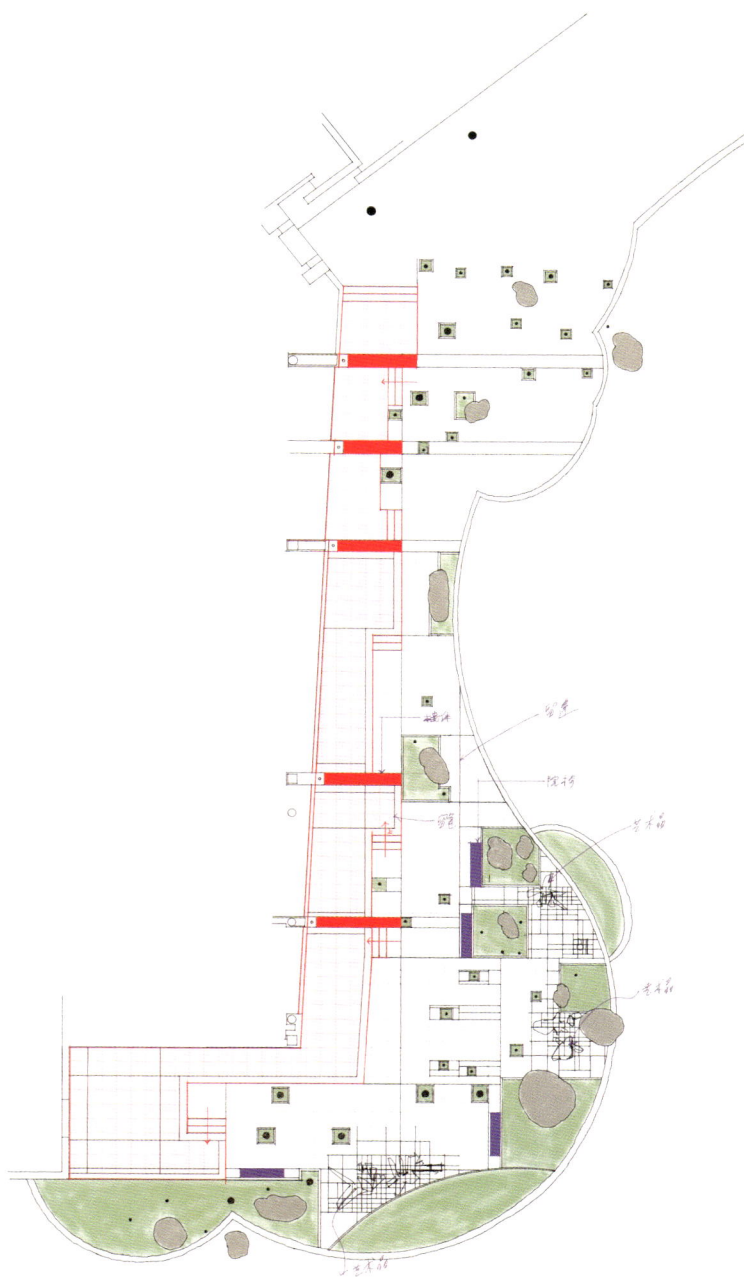

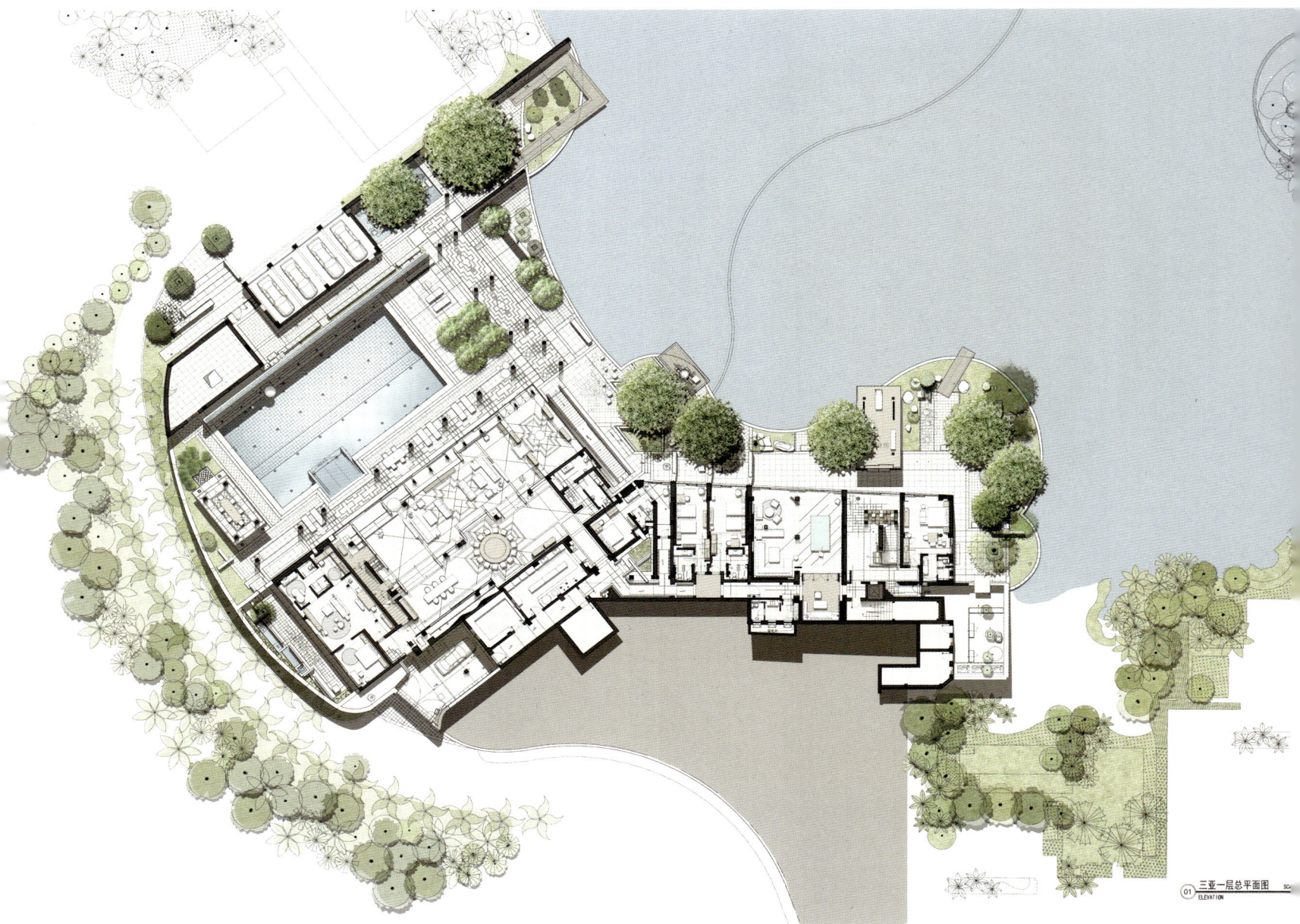

三亚一层总平面图
ELEVATION

在这项目里，希望处处都是景色、画面、光线、意境及实用的生活细节，所以很贪心地把这些要求都考虑到了设计中。

项目位于三亚海棠湾，是个度假型的住宅及小型私人会所酒店，共有12个房间，包括餐饮区、公共区和娱乐区等功能。最初接到项目时，还是一个未完成的建筑物，因此主要任务就是对其进行建筑和结构的改造，以及从室内到室外完成细节工程，交付使用。

During the reconstruction, we built a large platform in order to block the sun, and the horizontal lines of the platform block are easy to integrate with the environment, which it makes people interact better with nature. The huge roofing platform in the activity area can hold large-scale activities such as barbecue, cocktail party or wedding, and it not only greatly enhances the use of the site, but also can form a strong sense of rhythm with the indoor courtyard trails. The indoor structure which is exposed as much as possible can help to show the height of the space, and we extend it on this basis to form a more beautiful sense of rhythm.

　　三亚当地气候炎热，太阳毒辣，由于建筑地处海边，海风特别大，海水盐分高，腐蚀性强，所以材料的选择对于整个工程的质量非常重要，最终选用了山东白锈石、原木、质感漆三种耐久性比较高的装饰材料。

　　改造时，加建了大面积的平台，一是为了遮挡太阳，二是横线条的平台体块，很容易与环境融合在一起，让人与自然产生更好的情绪互动。活动区上巨大的屋面平台可以举行烧烤、酒会或婚礼等大型活动，大大地增强了场地的使用性，也可以跟室内的庭院小道形成强烈的节奏感。室内部分尽量裸露的结构形式，有助于显示空间的高度，在这基础上延伸它，形成更清晰的韵律感。

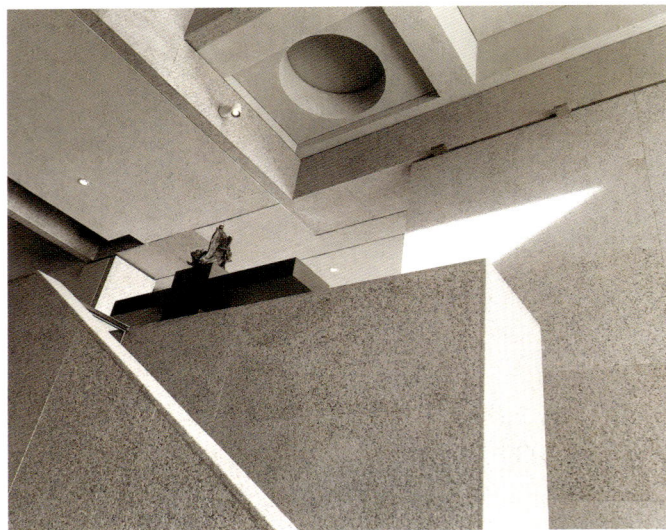

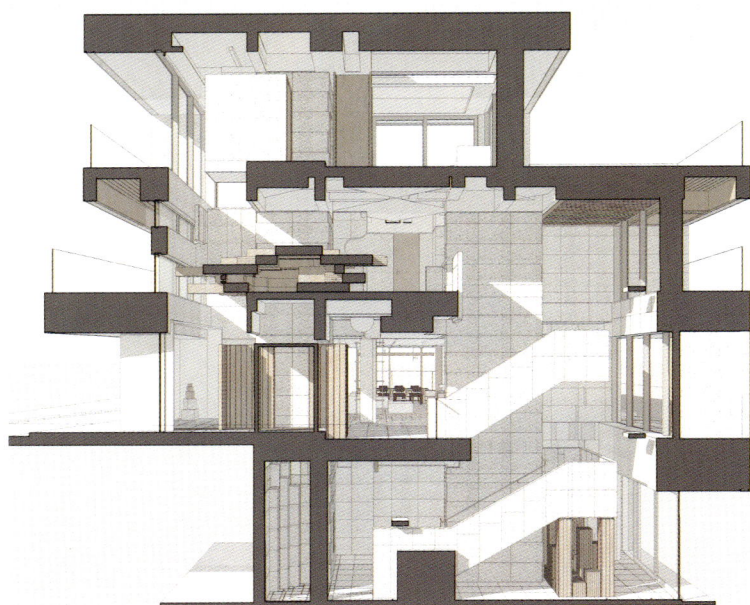

We put the sculptures, paintings, installations, lamps and even straw houses, streams and some different decorations in every corner, which can embody the rich and passionate, emotional culture of the courtyard. At the same time, the compositions mix all the contents together, so that there are the main line and peace in the noisy which can provide a place for people on holiday have a rest of mind.

每个角落里，设置了雕塑、绘画、灯具甚至稻草房、溪流等不同的配饰，体现了院落包容丰富、热情奔放的情感文化，同时，体块构成把所有的内容糅合在一起，又让喧闹中有了主线，有了宁静，给度假的人以心灵的休憩。

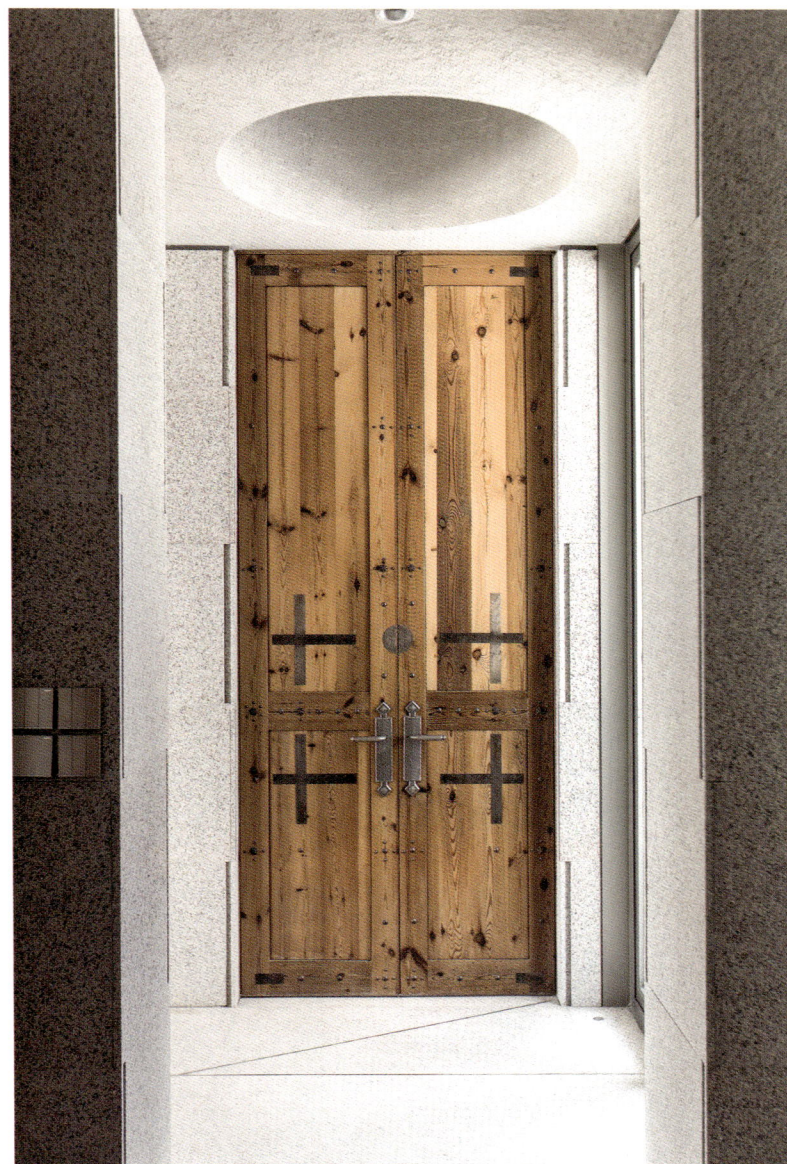

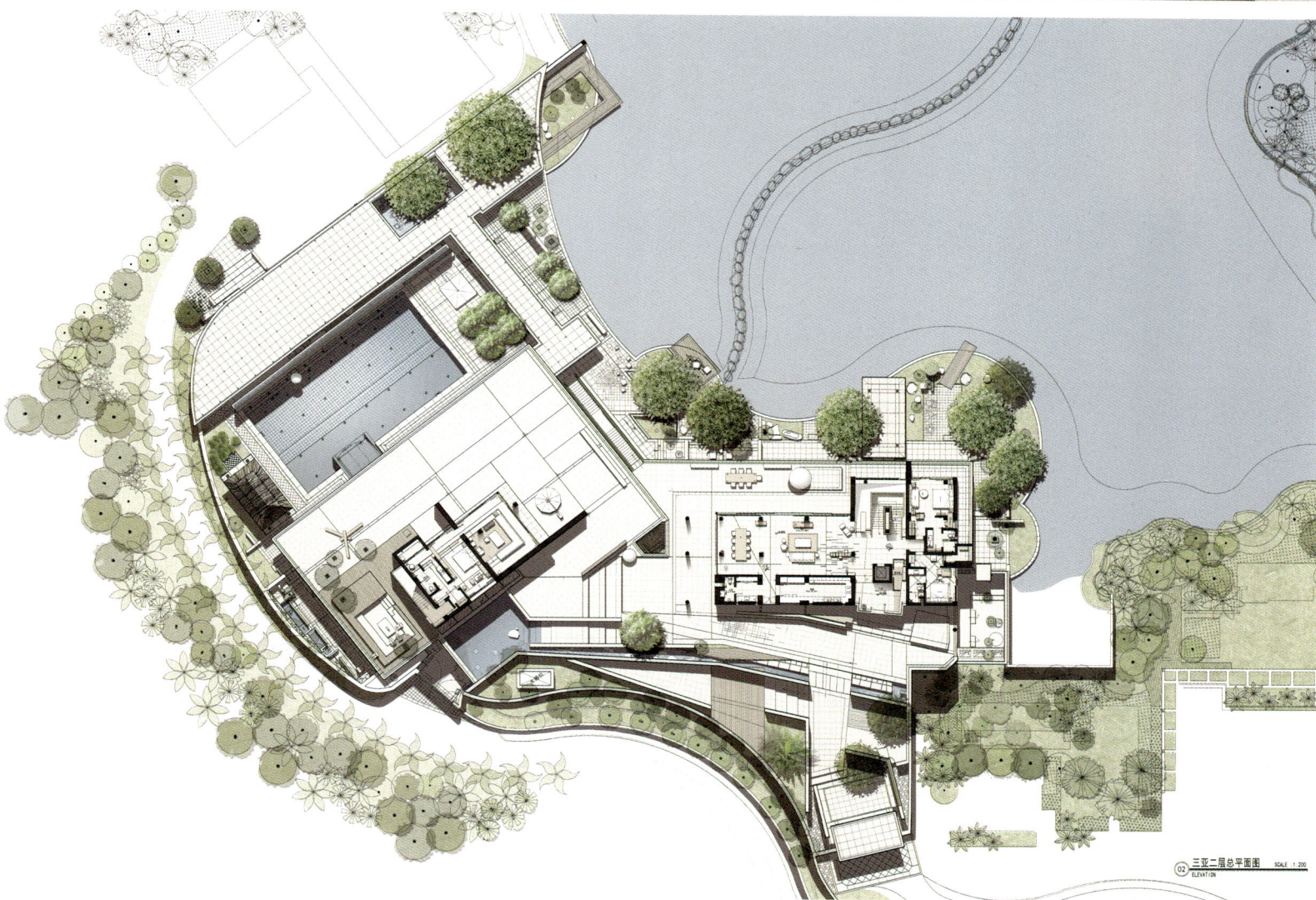

02 三亚二层总平面图   SCALE 1:200
ELEVATION

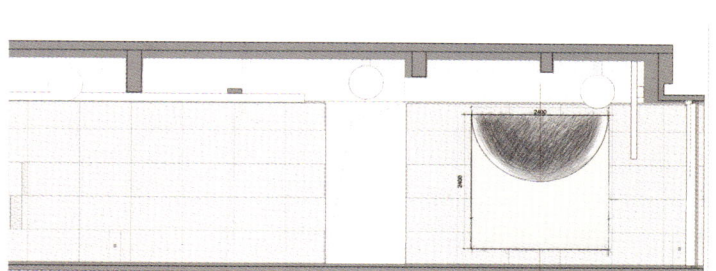

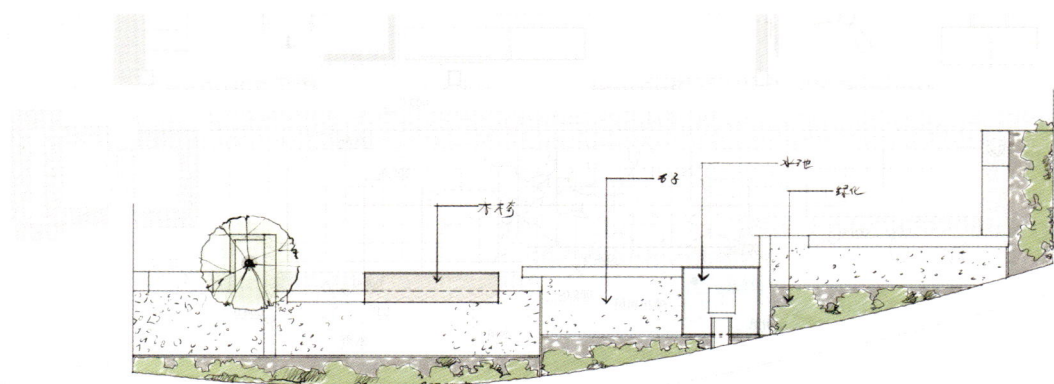

图书在版编目（ＣＩＰ）数据

设计对话 ： 亚太名师访谈 ／ 深圳视界文化传播有限
公司编． -- 北京 ： 中国林业出版社， 2018.2
   ISBN 978-7-5038-9417-6

Ⅰ．①设… Ⅱ．①深… Ⅲ．①设计师－访问记－亚洲
Ⅳ．① K833.057.2

中国版本图书馆 CIP 数据核字（2018）第 017941 号

编委会成员名单
策划制作：深圳视界文化传播有限公司（www.dvip-sz.com）
总 策 划：万　晶
编　　辑：杨珍琼
校　　对：陈劳平　尹丽斯
翻　　译：侯佳珍
装帧设计：叶一斌
联系电话：0755-82834960

中国林业出版社　·　建筑分社
策　　划：纪　亮
责任编辑：纪　亮　王思源

出版：中国林业出版社
（100009 北京西城区德内大街刘海胡同 7 号）
http://lycb.forestry.gov.cn/
电话：（010）8314 3518
发行：中国林业出版社
印刷：深圳市雅仕达印务有限公司
版次：2018 年 2 月第 1 版
印次：2018 年 2 月第 1 次
开本：235mm×335mm，1/16
印张：20
字数：300 千字
定价：428.00 元（USD 86.00）